Better Homes and Gardens®

1001
FULL-SIZE
PATTERNS
PROJECTS
& IDEAS

Better Homes and Gardens® Books
Des Moines, Iowa

1001 FULL-SIZE PATTERNS PROJECTS & IDEAS

Better Homes and Gardens® Books
An imprint of Meredith® Books

Editor: Carol Field Dahlstrom
Writer: Susan M. Banker
Designer: Angela Haupert Hoogensen
Copy Chief: Terri Fredrickson
Copy and Production Editor: Victoria Forlini
Editorial Operations Manager: Karen Schirm
Managers, Book Production: Pam Kvitne, Marjorie J. Schenkelberg, Rick von Holdt
Contributing Copy Editor: Arianna McKinney
Contributing Proofreaders: Sara Henderson, Sherri Schultz, Ann Terpstra
Photographers: Peter Krumhardt, Scott Little, Andy Lyons Cameraworks
Technical Illustrator: Chris Neubauer Graphics, Inc.
Electronic Production Coordinator: Paula Forest
Editorial and Design Assistants: Kaye Chabot, Mary Lee Gavin, Karen McFadden

Meredith® Books
Publisher and Editor in Chief: Linda Raglan Cunningham
Design Director: Matt Strelecki
Executive Editor, Food and Crafts: Jennifer Dorland Darling

Publisher: James D. Blume
Executive Director, Marketing: Jeffrey Myers
Executive Director, New Business Development: Todd M. Davis
Executive Director, Sales: Ken Zagor
Director, Operations: George A. Susral
Director, Production: Douglas M. Johnston
Business Director: Jim Leonard

Vice President and General Manager: Douglas J. Guendel

***Better Homes and Gardens*® Magazine**
Editor in Chief: Karol DeWulf Nickell

Meredith Publishing Group
President, Publishing Group: Stephen M. Lacy
Vice President-Publishing Director: Bob Mate

Meredith Corporation
Chairman and Chief Executive Officer: William T. Kerr

Chairman of the Executive Committee: E. T. Meredith III

it's all right here!

This book is full of choices. Chock-full of choices. We start by giving you project after project to fit any time of year and any event, complete with photos that show you how to make them. Then we offer patterns along with additional pattern possibilities. You can choose patterns that show you how to use leaf shapes, pumpkin faces, witch and ghost faces, cats, dogs, snowmen, snowflakes, Santas, stars, hearts, fruits and vegetables, Noah's ark animals, insects, paisley patterns, alphabets, numbers, zodiac signs, and so much more. Plus we offer additional ideas for how to use the projects and patterns. We include some patterns that give you color ideas and some black and white patterns for you to trace and transfer. All of the patterns are full size! You can always enlarge or reduce them on a copier if you want another size to fit your particular need.

We know that you'll think of even more uses for the patterns than we have. You know, like when you wanted to paint your toddler's bedroom with happy animals at the headboard but didn't have any animal patterns to refer to. **Now you have plenty.** Or the time when you had the Scouts over to make Valentines and they all needed help drawing or cutting a heart—and you weren't sure you could draw one yourself. **Now you have dozens!** And of course when you were eager to make a birthday card for your best friend but couldn't come up with any birthday design ideas. **Now the inspiration is endless!**

We know you'll enjoy this book of 1001 projects, patterns, and ideas we've shared for every season and every reason. So start making your fun-to-do crafting choices. It's all right here.

Carol Field Dahlstrom

table of contents

chapter 5—pages 154–227
spring and summer
Flowers, fish, and so-silly bugs are just some of the patterns you'll find in this sunshiny chapter. Use these warm-weather designs to paint tiles, an egg, a sink, and a stool. Or try etching glasses—the sky is the limit with dozens of patterns on hand.

chapter 6—pages 228–261
alphabets and numbers
With different styles of letters and numbers to use, you can personalize just about anything. Paint a set of cups, quilt a pillow, or make blankets, door hangers, or ornaments for you and those special people in your life.

chapter 7—pages 262–281
geometrics, stars, and the zodiac
Your crafting techniques will really take flight with such an array of fun patterns. Paint a wood piece in the shape of a star or make an intricate top that spins. Sew a bright table runner with zodiac signs or cut paper stars to hang throughout your home. Your sign awaits!

halloween and autumn

*Celebrate autumn with oodles of ideas
for beautifully painted and carved
pumpkins, Halloween curtains,
leaf-embellished place mats, and many*

*more entertaining projects to illuminate
your house. Choose from dozens of
patterns to make autumn projects with
your own style.*

leaf-laden pumpkins

An elegant display outdoors or in, these pumpkin candleholders can delight visitors all autumn long.

supplies
Pumpkins
Sharp knife
Candles
Drill and 1-inch hole saw
Tracing paper
Pencil
Scissors
Tape
Metallic gold spray paint
Acrylic paints
Paintbrushes
Tube glitter paint

what to do

1 For each pumpkin, cut off the stem, if desired. For candleholders, using a drill and a 1-inch hole saw, drill a hole in the pumpkin top. If necessary, use a knife to cut a larger hole to fit a candle. Wipe the pumpkin clean.

2 Trace the desired leaf patterns, *pages 10–11*. Cut out the shapes and tape them to the pumpkin.

3 Spray on gold paint, covering the leaf patterns. Let the paint dry. Remove the patterns.

4 Fill in the leaf shapes by blending acrylic paints (pink into purple, yellow into green, and orange into red), or paint the leaves solid colors. Let the paint dry.

5 Outline the leaf shapes with glitter paint.

NOTE: *Never leave a burning candle unattended.*

LEAF-LADEN PUMPKINS
PATTERNS

A favorite stenciling pattern from two centuries ago, this weeping willow is stunning carved on an autumn pumpkin. Or select from the patterns on pages 14–17 to create a distinctive pumpkin for your decorating scheme.

weeping willow pumpkin

supplies

Pumpkin
Sharp knife
Spoon or ice cream scoop
Tracing paper
Pencil
Candle

what to do

1 Cut around the pumpkin stem to remove the top. Using the spoon or scoop, clean out the seeds and membrane.

2 Trace a pattern from pages 14–17. Trace the pattern onto the pumpkin with a pencil, redrawing lines as necessary to darken.

3 Use a sharp knife to carve the design, cutting just deep enough to expose the translucent flesh without cutting all the way through. Place a candle in the pumpkin. A lighted candle allows the design to show more clearly.

NOTE: *Never leave a burning candle unattended.*

WEEPING WILLOW PUMPKIN
PATTERN

11 more ways to use these pumpkin patterns:

- *Use a fine black permanent marker to draw the patterns on the outside of an uncarved pumpkin.*
- *Using dots of paint to follow the patterns, draw the shapes on a plain place mat.*
- *Copy and reduce the desired Halloween pattern on a copy machine and glue the design to a folded piece of black card stock to create a striking card.*
- *Place a piece of tracing paper over the design and number the "dots." Give the tracing paper to a child to connect the dots.*
- *Transfer the pattern to stencil paper, cut out the holes, and use as a stencil pattern for decorating walls or fabrics.*
- *Reduce the patterns as needed to paint on odd-shaped gourds.*
- *Use the patterns as a guide to embroider a pillow top using satin stitches and lazy daisy stitches.*
- *Use the cat pattern as a guide to add a jeweled pattern to the side of a canvas tote bag.*
- *Transfer the tree motif to a scrapbook page that focuses on a family tree.*
- *Use a crafts knife to cut the bat design from black paper. Back the cutout with white paper for a striking Halloween party invitation.*
- *Copy a design onto a shirt and paint in the areas with fabric paint.*

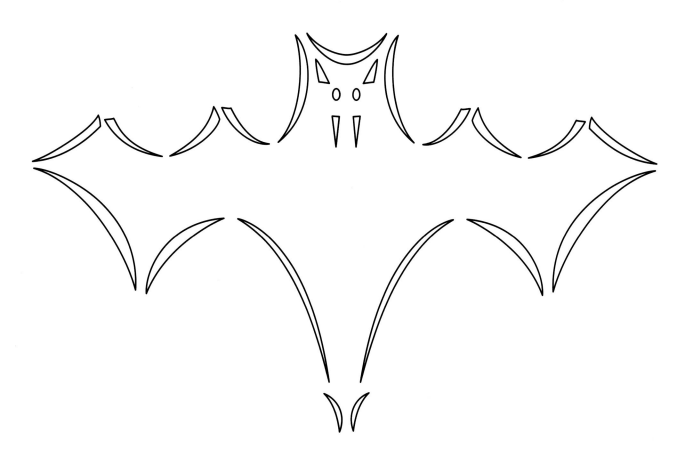

ALTERNATIVE PUMPKIN
PATTERNS

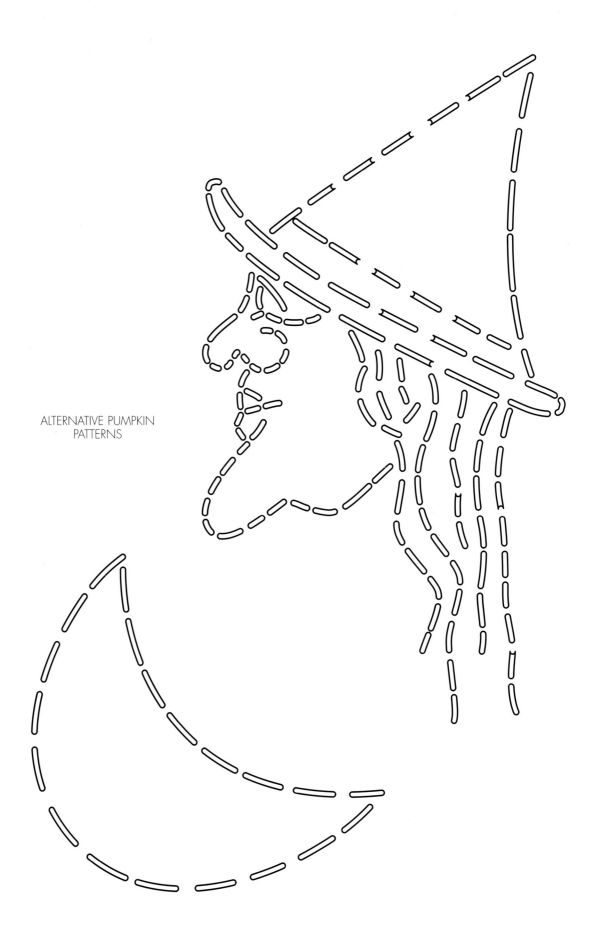

ALTERNATIVE PUMPKIN
PATTERNS

pumpkin patterns

ALTERNATIVE PUMPKIN
PATTERNS

bewitching curtains

Tracing paper; pencil
Plastic template material
Crafts knife; flat panel tab-top
  curtains in off-white or ecru
Acrylic paint in black or white
Small flat paintbrushes
Paper towel
Black tube paint
Beading needle and thread
Seed beads in black, green,
  or tan for eyes

what to do

1 Trace the desired patterns, *pages 20–21,* to template material. Cut out the shapes and solid black areas with a crafts knife. Trace the templates in various positions on the curtain (see Photo A, *right*).

2 Use a dry-brush technique and follow the traced lines to paint the bats and cats black and to paint the ghosts white. To dry-brush, dab off most of the paint onto a paper towel; then paint the fabric design (see Photo B). Too much paint on the brush will cause it to bleed. Hang or lay the curtain flat while the paint dries. If desired, use black tube paint to draw in face details and to outline the shapes.

3 Hand-stitch two seed bead eyes onto each bat, cat, or ghost, knotting thread ends on the back of the curtain.

A

B

Affix frightful flair
to your windows
by stenciling
Halloween motifs
on tab-top curtains.

try these ideas

9 *more ways to use these curtain patterns:*

- *Paint the designs on a plastic pail for a trick-or-treat candy holder.*
- *Appliqué the designs on a canvas tote bag.*
- *Paint the symbols on a premade pillow using fabric paint.*
- *Cut the designs from paper to make party invitations or note cards.*
- *Enlarge one of the patterns and paint it on a sweatshirt.*
- *Transfer the designs to a pumpkin and cut out using the technique on* page 13.
- *Stencil the designs on a flat area rug.*
- *Cut the shapes from paper, punch a hole in the top of each one, string thread through the holes, and hang the ornaments from doorways, ceiling fans, or light fixtures.*
- *Make a wood Welcome sign and paint the desired themes as a border.*

curtain patterns

BEWITCHING
CURTAINS PATTERNS
AND ALTERNATIVE
CURTAIN PATTERNS

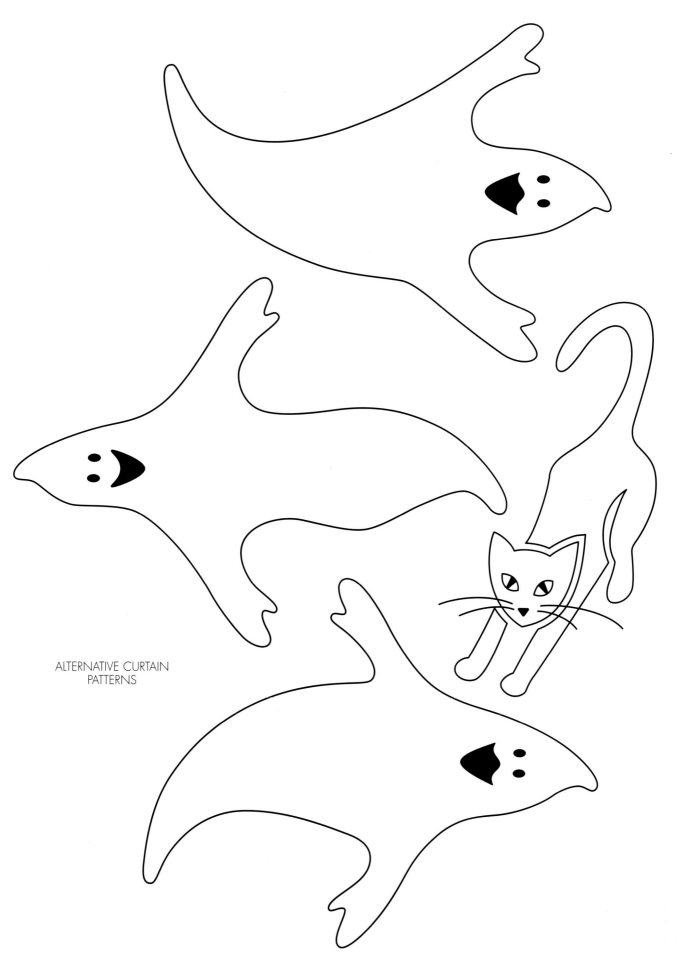

ALTERNATIVE CURTAIN
PATTERNS

jack o. lantern pillow

This wide-eyed and toothy-grinned pumpkin livens up a pillow top. Pick your favorite character from the patterns on pages 24–27.

supplies

*Tracing paper; pencil; scissors
Felt pieces in bright green,
    orange, and yellow
Embroidery floss in black,
    blue, lime green, orange,
    and purple
2 large black seed beads
8½-inch square of purple felt
Two 12-inch squares of blue felt
Needle; white thread
Fiberfill*

what to do

1. Trace and cut out the desired patterns, *pages 24–27*. The four small designs can be placed in a grid formation on the pillow.
2. Trace around the pattern pieces onto coordinating pieces of felt. Cut out the felt shapes.
3. Using blanket stitches (see *page 25*) and embroidery floss, sew the eyes, nose, and mouth on the pumpkin. Use white thread to sew a seed bead in the center of each eye, making several small spoke-like stitches.
4. Blanket-stitch the pumpkin to the purple felt piece using blue floss. Center the purple felt square on a blue square. Blanket-stitch it in place using green floss. Blanket-stitch the stem in place using green floss.
5. Leaving an opening for stuffing, stitch pillow front to other blue felt square using blanket stitches. Stuff pillow with fiberfill. Stitch the opening closed.
6. Cut four 6-inch orange squares for bows. Pinch the centers together; tack them to the pillow top.

---

try these ideas

4 more ways to use the pumpkin pillow patterns:

- *Appliqué a Halloween motif on an orange T-shirt.*
- *Paint the designs on wood to make yard stakes.*
- *Trace and cut a design from colorful paper to decoupage on the top of a small round table.*
- *Enlarge the patterns, trace on craft foam, and cut out to make place mats.*

STEM PATTERN

JACK O. LANTERN
PILLOW PATTERNS

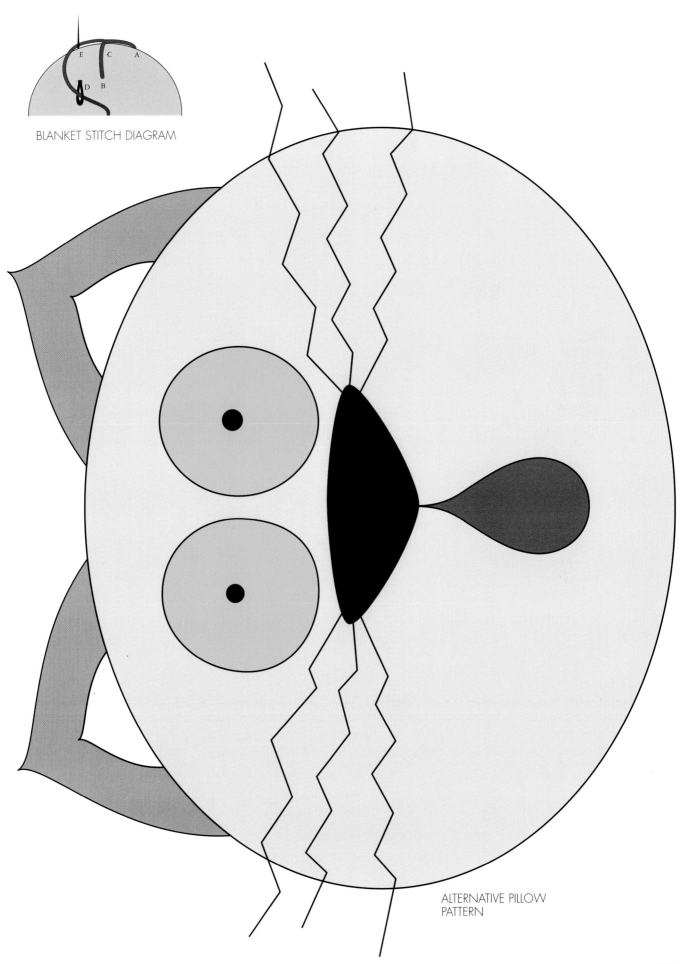

BLANKET STITCH DIAGRAM

ALTERNATIVE PILLOW
PATTERN

25

ALTERNATIVE PILLOW
PATTERN

ALTERNATIVE PILLOW PATTERNS

27

mealtime mat

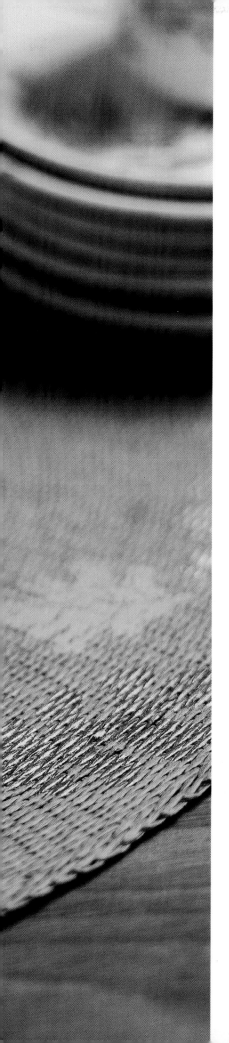

Pick your favorite fall-time designs to spruce up place mats. We used leaves for an autumn table setting. Find plenty of designs on pages 30–31 to suit your taste any time of the year.

supplies

Place mat
Tracing paper; transfer paper
Pencil; crafts knife
Stencil material
Disposable plate
Acrylic paints in desired colors
Stencil brush; black paint pen

what to do

1 Trace the desired patterns from *pages 30–31.* Use transfer paper to copy patterns to the stencil material. On a protected work surface, cut out the shapes with a crafts knife.

2 Place a small amount of the desired paint colors on a plate, separated enough to avoid mixing paint colors. Dip the stencil brush into the paint and dab off excess on the plate or a paper towel. Position the stencil on the place mat and dab on paint through the opening as shown in Photo A, *right.* Reposition the stencil and repeat to make a border along the edge of the place mat. Let the paint dry.

3 Detail or add dots and lines to the stencil designs using a black paint pen as shown in Photo B.

A

B

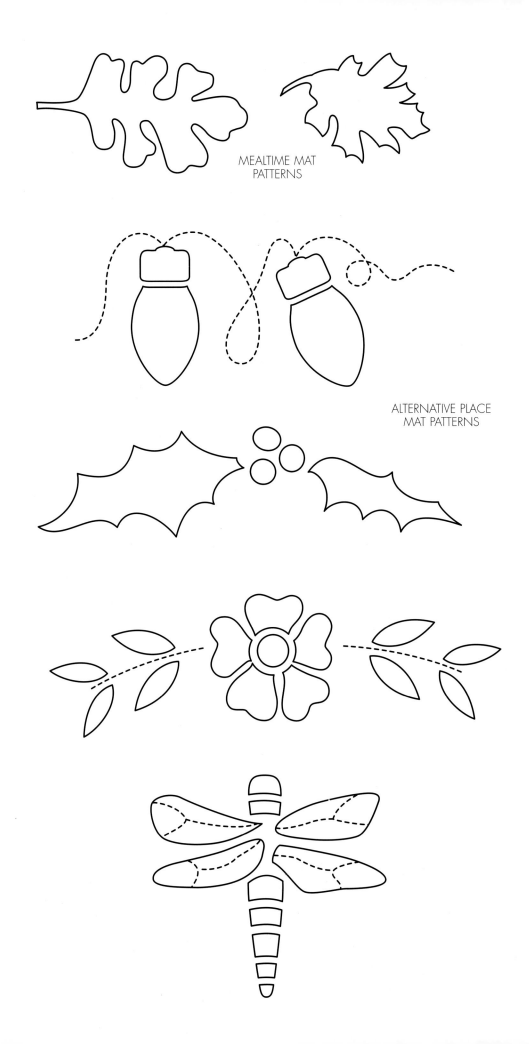

MEALTIME MAT
PATTERNS

ALTERNATIVE PLACE
MAT PATTERNS

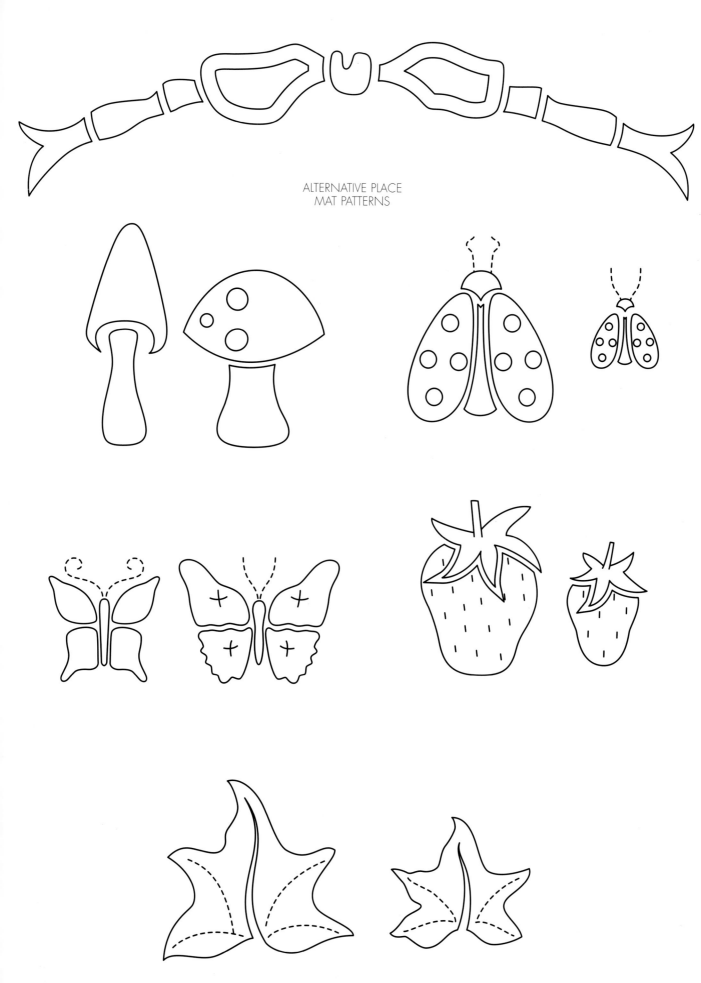

ALTERNATIVE PLACE
MAT PATTERNS

31

christmas and winter

*The holidays sparkle with handmade
accents that spread good cheer.
This festive chapter offers ideas for
beautiful ornaments, clever tree skirts,*

too-pretty-to-open package trims, and
merry table settings—plus a sleigh full of
patterns to create all the seasonal magic
your heart can hold.

frosted flame

A flea-market find takes on a holiday glow when you decorate it with mini etched Christmas themes.

supplies
*Clear laminating film; pencil
Crafts knife; glass cleaner
Glass votive; plastic gloves
Etching cream; paintbrush*

what to do

1 Trace the desired designs, *opposite,* directly onto laminating film. Cut out the designs from the film with a crafts knife.

2 Clean the votive with glass cleaner that does not leave a film; let dry. Arrange the designs on the votive. Firmly press them in place by sealing the edges with a fingernail.

3 Wearing plastic gloves and working in a well-ventilated area, brush etching cream on the votive, following the manufacturer's directions, covering all areas evenly. Let stand for five minutes. Thoroughly rinse the votive with water to remove the cream. Peel off the laminating film.

FROSTED FLAME PATTERNS

Accent a set of ornaments with beads and tiny decorative stitches, choosing from the assorted patterns on pages 38–39 to make a tree full.

supplies

Tracing paper; pencil
Scissors
Felt in white, black, blue, green, gold, light gray, orange, and red
Thick white crafts glue
Poly-fil
Seed beads in amber, black, red, and medium green
Embroidery floss in black, light green, medium green, and gold
Trims, such as beads, sequins, and buttons
Hanging loop and trims, such as cord, ribbon, and rickrack
Pinking shears

what to do

1 Trace and cut out the desired patterns from pages 38–39.

2 **For the snowman,** from felt cut two black hats, two white bodies, and blue scarf pieces. Fringe the scarf by snipping the ends with scissors. Glue the scarf to the snowman. Cut out and glue on felt pieces for the black mouth and the orange carrot nose. For eyes, use black seed beads to anchor larger beads. Blanket-stitch the snowman bodies together, leaving an opening at the top. Stuff with poly-fil; glue the opening closed. Trim the black hat if desired. Glue hat pieces to the snowman, inserting the hanging loop between the hat layers.

3 **For the drum,** from felt cut two drum shapes from green, upper and lower bands from black, and a drum top from gold. Glue the black and gold pieces to the drum. Glue or stitch trim on the drum. Sew on five decorative beads or buttons to finish. Blanket-stitch (see diagram, *page 38*) drum pieces together, inserting poly-fil and a hanging loop before stitching completely closed.

4 **For the candy cane,** from felt cut two white canes and five red stripes. Glue stripes to the white cane. Sew green seed beads along red edges. Blanket-stitch the front and back of the cane together, inserting poly-fil and a hanging loop before stitching completely closed.

continued on page 38

5 **For the star,** from felt cut two black stars, one blue rectangle, and one red diamond, cutting the blue and red pieces with pinking shears if desired. Fold the red diamond in half; cut out inner diamond. Glue the blue and red pieces to one black star. From felt snip black dots and glue them to the red diamond. Sew beads to the center. Blanket-stitch star layers together; at each star tip, thread a red bead onto needle and sew through bead twice to secure. Insert poly-fil and a hanging loop before stitching completely closed.

6 **For the bell,** from felt cut two bells from blue, a wide band from light gray, a narrow band from orange, and a cap from black. Glue the bands together; blanket-stitch with light green floss. Sew a bead and button to the center of the orange band and sequins or beads at each side; secure with amber seed beads. Glue the band on the bell; blanket-stitch with medium green floss. Sew amber seed beads on the gray band. Glue black cap on bell. Blanket-stitch the bell layers together, inserting poly-fil and a hanging loop before stitching completely closed.

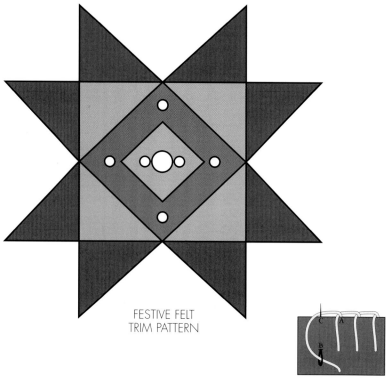

FESTIVE FELT TRIM PATTERN

BLANKET STITCH

ALTERNATIVE TRIM PATTERNS

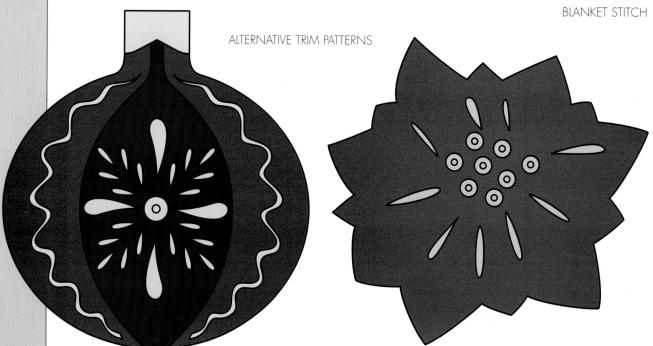

FESTIVE FELT TRIM PATTERNS

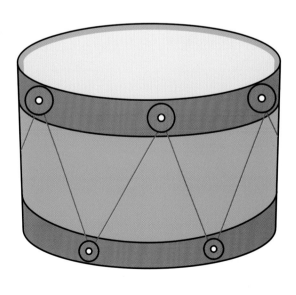

Top a holiday package gracefully by attaching a layered felt poinsettia to a ribbon. For more seasonal flower toppers, see pages 44–45.

supplies

Tracing paper; pencil; scissors
Fusible adhesive
Felt in dark green, gold, light green, and red
Metallic gold sewing machine thread; sewing thread; needle
7 metallic round gold beads
7 metallic gold cupped flower beads; ribbon

what to do

1 Trace and cut out the poinsettia or other flower patterns, *pages 42–45.* Trace the patterns to the paper side of fusible adhesive.

2 Fuse the adhesive to red felt; cut out the shapes. Fuse each poinsettia shape to green felt pieces. Trim the green felt just beyond the red edges. Cut the flower center from gold felt.

3 Using metallic gold thread and a decorative sewing machine stitch, outline-stitch along the red leaves.

4 Layer the poinsettias to show all the leaves, with the larger layer beneath. Tack the flower center in place.

5 Using sewing thread and a needle, hand-sew through the flower center and the two layers of leaves, attaching a cupped flower bead and round bead with each stitch. Wrap a ribbon around a package and sew the poinsettia topper to the ribbon.

---

try these ideas

***5** more ways to use the package topper patterns:*

- *Trace and paint a flower on a hatbox lid for a decorative storage container.*
- *Reduce a pattern and transfer it to the side of a 3-wick candle. Outline the design with upholstery tacks.*
- *Appliqué a flower to the side of a cloth tote bag.*
- *Tack motifs cut from felt to the lower edge of a plain window valance.*
- *Sew felt flowers to plain felt Christmas stockings.*

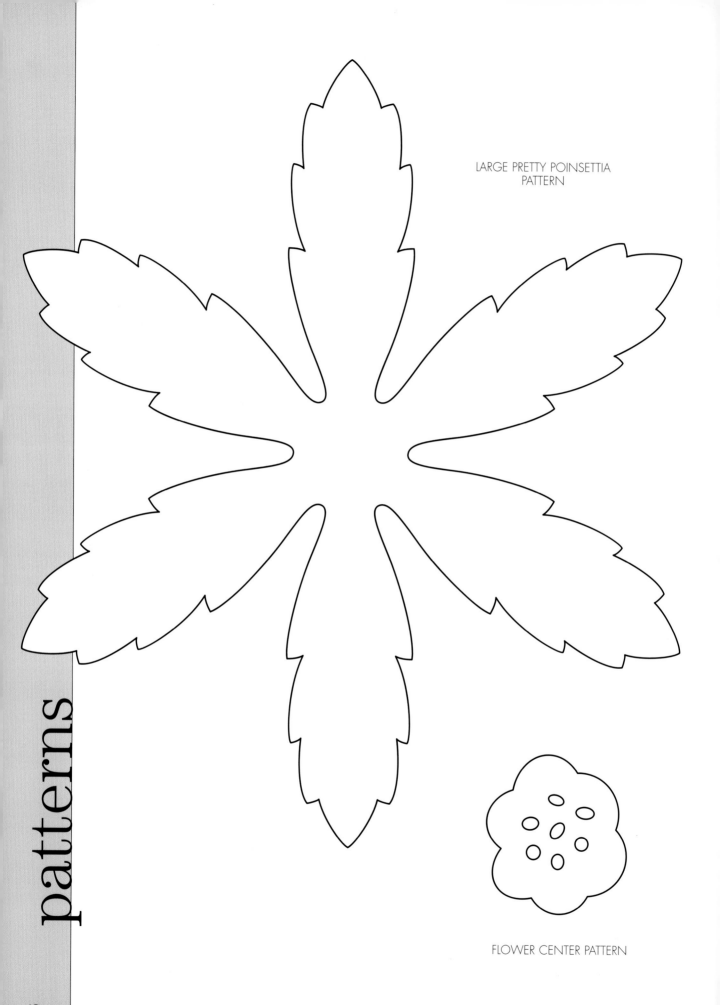

LARGE PRETTY POINSETTIA
PATTERN

FLOWER CENTER PATTERN

SMALL PRETTY POINSETTIA
PATTERN

6 *more ways to use the package topper patterns:*

- *Tack felt flowers to the edge of a coordinating afghan.*
- *Cut the designs from paper to make greeting cards.*
- *Cut the motifs from wood and paint them for ornaments.*
- *Machine-stitch fabric designs to a sweatshirt.*
- *Enlarge one of the designs to make a Christmas tree topper.*
- *Trace the designs onto flattened oven-bake clay, such as Sculpey, to make holiday coasters.*

ALTERNATIVE PACKAGE TOPPER
LARGE FOUR-PETAL POSY PATTERN

ALTERNATIVE PACKAGE TOPPER
SMALL FOUR-PETAL POSY PATTERN

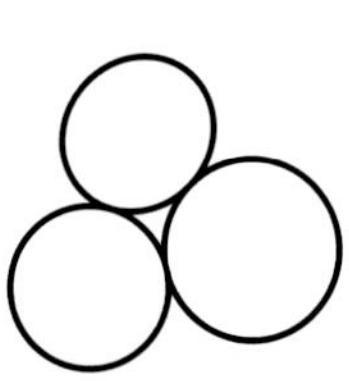

FLOWER CENTER PATTERN

FLOWER CENTER
PATTERN

ALTERNATIVE PACKAGE TOPPER
LARGE AND SMALL DAISY PATTERNS

ALTERNATIVE
PACKAGE TOPPER
LARGE AND
SMALL CLOVER
PATTERNS

FLOWER CENTER PATTERN

45

snowmen sensations

Whether frolicking on cookie containers or glass ornaments, these friendly fellows will add cheer to the season.

cool cookie containers

supplies

Tracing paper; pencil
Cookie containers in red
and white (available in
crafts stores)
Stiffened felt pieces in red,
white and bright green
Double-stick tape
Pinking shears; paper punch
Thick white crafts glue
Black paint pen

what to do

1 Trace the desired patterns, *pages 48–49.* Use the patterns to cut a snowman from white felt. Center and adhere the snowman with double-stick tape to the top of a cookie container. From green and red felt, cut out the nose, scarf, buttons, mittens, and earmuff or hat.

2 Glue the pieces to the snowman.

3 Use pinking shears to cut a ¼-inch-wide strip from the length of stiffened felt. Apply a strip of double-stick tape to the rim of the lid. Aligning the flat edge of the felt with the rim, press the strip to the tape.

4 Punch dots from white felt. Glue the dots to the sides of the tin. Use the black paint pen to draw arms, eyes, and mouth.

continued on page 48

jolly fellow ornaments
supplies
Flattened round clear glass
ornaments

Paint markers, such as
Uchida, in black, green, red,
and white
White glitter

what to do
1 Place an ornament over a reduced copy of a snowman pattern. Draw the snowman on the front of the ornament, outlining it in black. Color in the design. To prevent colors from bleeding, let each color dry before coloring adjacent sections.

2 Remove the ornament cap hanger. Pour glitter in the ornament; replace the cap.

SNOWMEN SENSATIONS
PATTERNS

SNOWMEN SENSATIONS
PATTERNS

49

ever-bright branches

supplies for the garland

Wide, wired white satin ribbon on a spool; pencil
Scissors; fabric paints in green, purple, red, and turquoise
2 wood beads with wide openings for each banner
Paintbrush
Acrylic paints in green, purple, red, and turquoise

supplies for the ornaments

Tracing paper; pencil; scissors
⅛-inch-thick white craft foam
Spray adhesive; metallic papers; utility knife
White fabric paint; white glitter; paper punch; ribbon

what to do

1 **For garland,** unwind a spool of wide white ribbon. Using a pencil and *page 55* as a guide, lightly write phrases on the ribbon, allowing approximately 6 to 12 inches of blank space before and after the phrases. Fold the ribbon in half lengthwise; cut the ribbon ends diagonally to form a V-shape. Trace the phrases with fabric paint. Let dry.

2 Place beads on the handle of a paintbrush to hold them while painting. Basecoat beads with acrylic paint. Let dry. To paint dots, dip the end of a paintbrush handle in paint and dot onto bead. Let dry. Slip a bead onto ribbon at each end.

3 **For ornaments,** trace and cut out the patterns, *pages 52–54.*

4 In a well-ventilated work area, spray the back of metallic paper with a heavy coat of adhesive. Adhere to the white foam.

5 Trace shapes onto foamed metallic paper; cut out with a utility knife. For shapes with two colors, such as the gift packages, cut the second color from paper, apply adhesive to the back, and adhere it to the ornament.

6 Outline the shapes with white fabric paint; sprinkle the wet paint with white glitter. Let dry. Shake off excess glitter. Punch a hole in the ornament; loop ribbon through the hole and tie it in a knot for hanging.

These playful ornaments and garlands awaken childhood memories of magical Christmases past. See the patterns on pages 52–55.

EVER-BRIGHT BRANCHES
ORNAMENT PATTERNS

EVER-BRIGHT BRANCHES
ORNAMENT PATTERNS

53

EVER-BRIGHT BRANCHES
ORNAMENT PATTERN

try these ideas

6 *more ways to use the ornament and garland patterns:*

- *Cut the shapes from felt and stitch to a Christmas tree skirt using blanket stitches.*
- *Cut the star or moon shapes from a paper bag; back the opening with colored cellophane.*
- *Make gift tags or package toppers from colored paper.*
- *Tie several reindeer ornaments together to make a garland.*
- *Trace the verse,* opposite, *on vellum to make a holiday card.*
- *Appliqué felt package motifs on a tablecloth.*

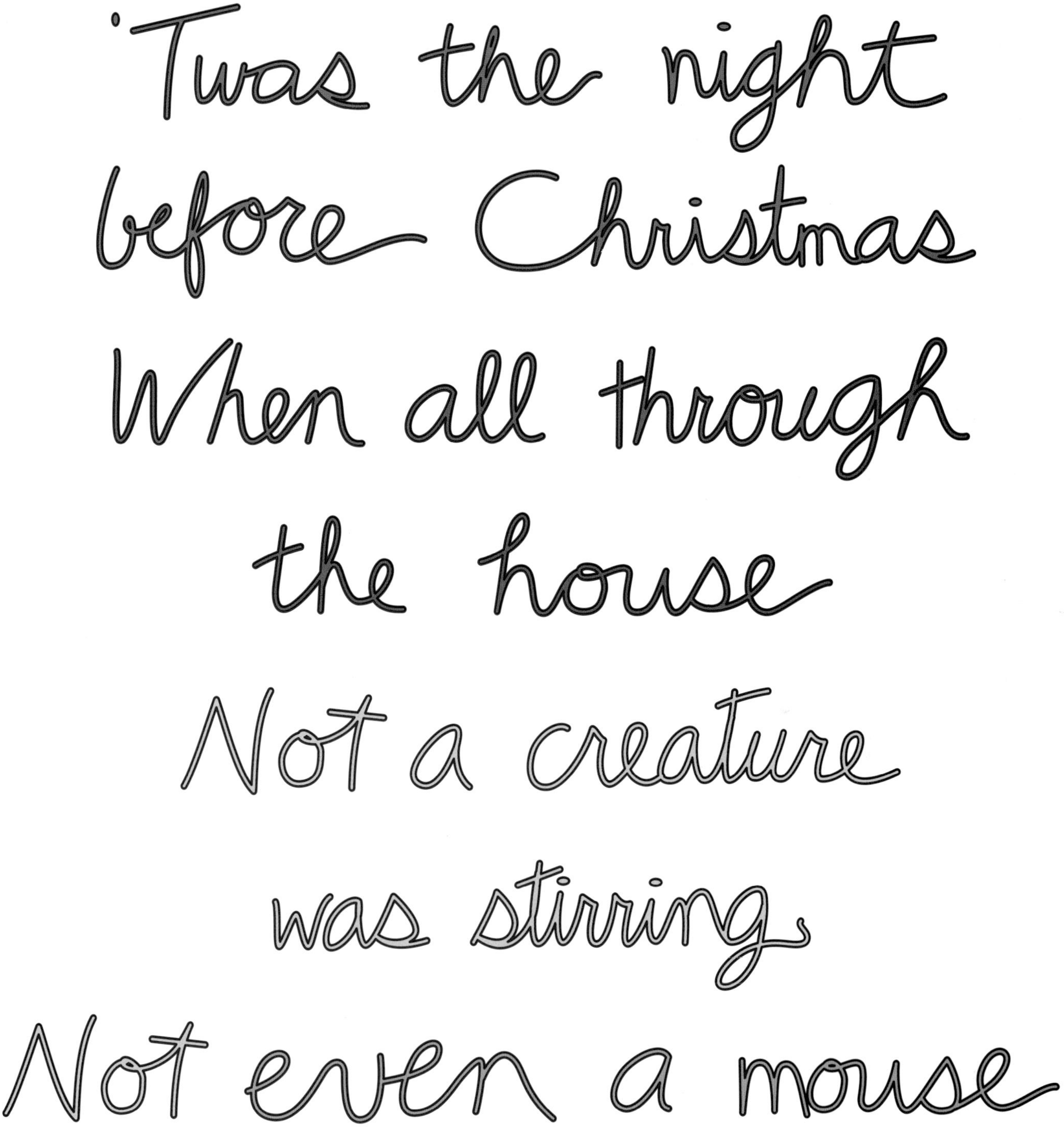

'Twas the night
before Christmas
When all through
the house
Not a creature
was stirring,
Not even a mouse

EVER-BRIGHT BRANCHES
GARLAND PATTERN

Fluffy fabric snowmen encircle a starry night sky. Utilize the fun collection of patterns on pages 58–61 to make a winsome tree skirt.

supplies

Black felt circle in desired tree skirt size; scissors
Embroidery floss in black, gold, and coordinating colors
Needle
Tracing paper; pencil
Off-white pile fabric
Felt in pumpkin orange, gold, and green; small buttons

what to do

1 Cut a 5-inch hole from the center of a black felt circle. Cut an opening from the skirt edge to the center.

2 Blanket-stitch (see diagram, *page 59*) with gold floss around the edges and opening.

3 Trace and cut out patterns, *pages 58–61*. Transfer and cut out the patterns from pile fabric and felt.

4 Using matching thread or floss and tiny stitches, tack the snowmen in place. Sew on buttons, knotting the thread on top.

continued on page 58

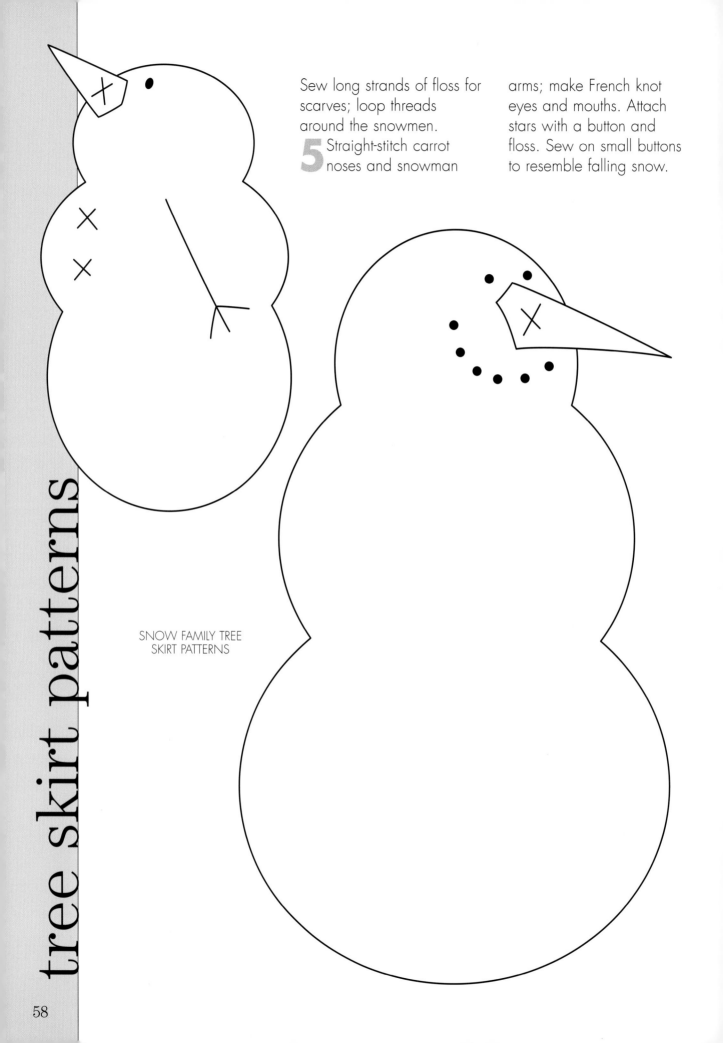

Sew long strands of floss for scarves; loop threads around the snowmen.

5 Straight-stitch carrot noses and snowman arms; make French knot eyes and mouths. Attach stars with a button and floss. Sew on small buttons to resemble falling snow.

SNOW FAMILY TREE
SKIRT PATTERNS

tree skirt patterns

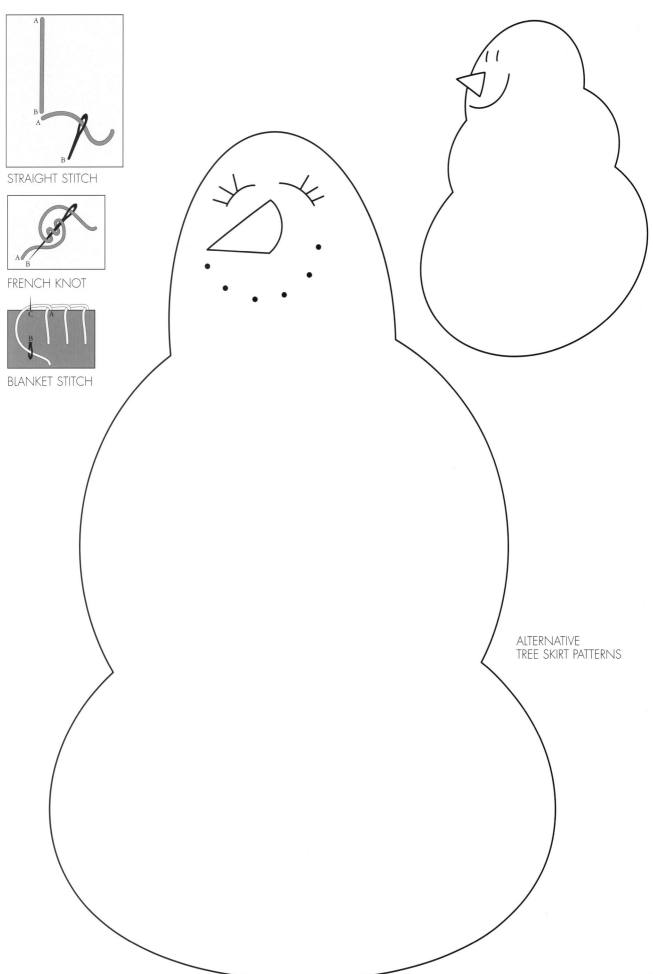

STRAIGHT STITCH

FRENCH KNOT

BLANKET STITCH

ALTERNATIVE
TREE SKIRT PATTERNS

59

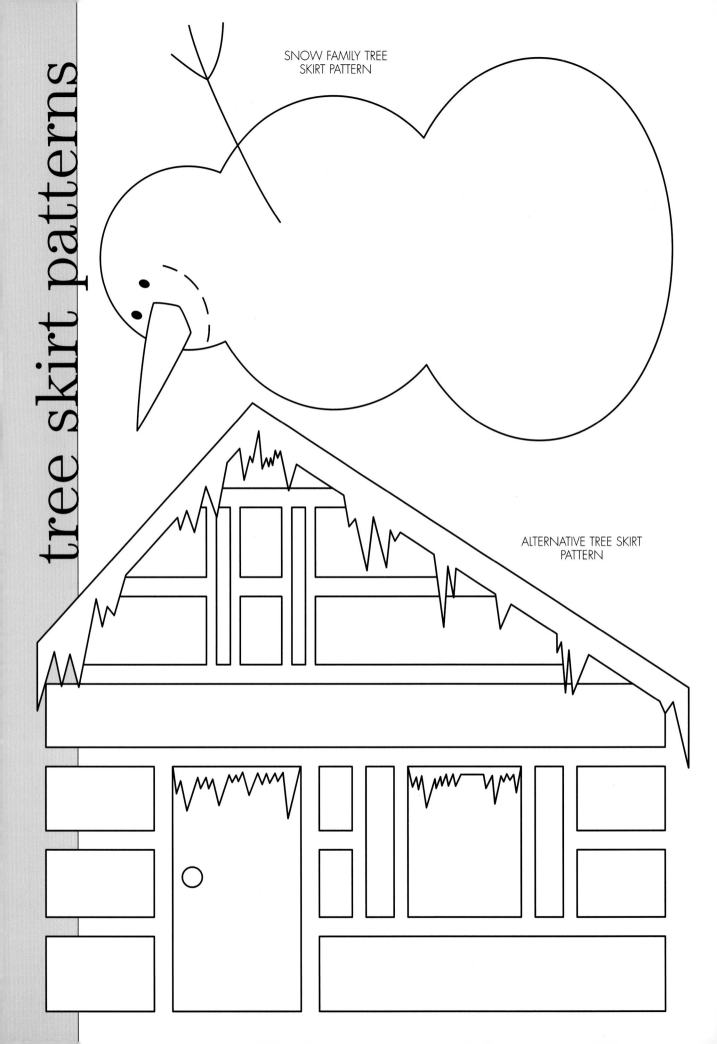

tree skirt patterns

SNOW FAMILY TREE
SKIRT PATTERN

ALTERNATIVE TREE SKIRT
PATTERN

SNOW FAMILY TREE SKIRT
PATTERNS

clay christmas ornaments

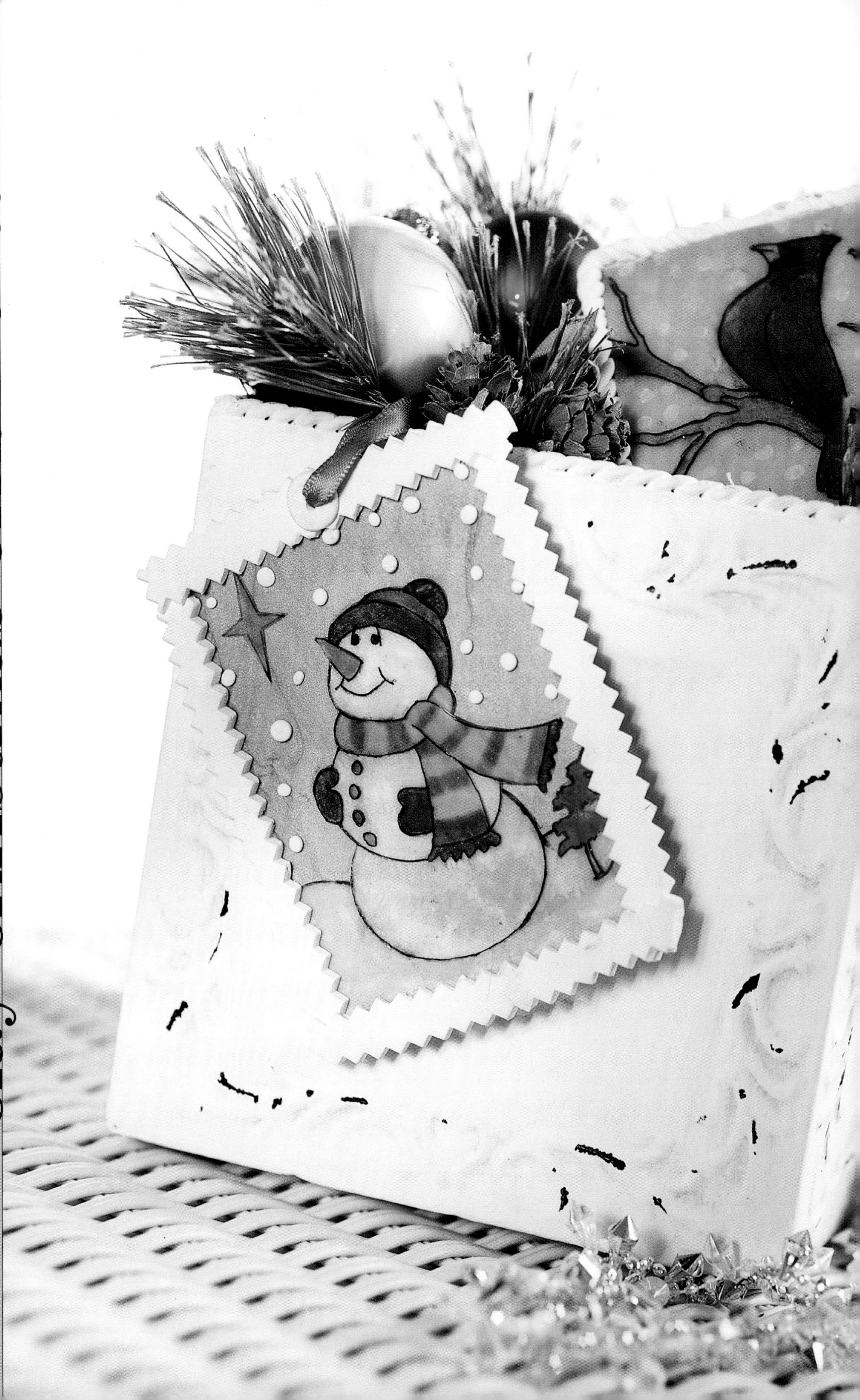

A joy to make, give, and hang on the tree, these dear decorations will bring merriment at tree-trimming time. Make use of the selection on pages 64–65.

A

B

C

supplies

Photocopy of patterns (pages 64–65) other than ink jet, which will smear
Artist-quality colored pencils
Liquid Sculpey; paintbrush
Glass baking dish with flat bottom
Scissors; crafts knife
Oven-bake clay, such as Sculpey, in desired colors
Decorative edge scissors
Toothpick; ribbon

what to do

1 Neatly color in the photocopy with colored pencils (see Photo A) *above right,* so it will transfer well.

2 Using a paintbrush or your finger, spread a thin layer of Liquid Sculpey over the colored surface of the paper (see Photo B). When Sculpey is applied too thick, the image is weak. Place wet side up in a glass baking dish. Bake in preheated oven according to the product manufacturer's directions. Remove and let cool. The baked clay should feel firm, dry, and rubbery.

continued on page 64

3 Soak the baked drawing, paper side up, in water (see Photo C, *page 63*). Very gently rub the paper from the firm clay surface. Gently pat dry.

4 Trim the image to the outline.

5 To make a clay backing piece or frame, roll out desired color of clay to ⅟16 to ⅛ inch thickness. Spread a very small amount of Liquid Sculpey on the back (former paper side) of the image, just enough to make it wet. Press on the rolled-out background clay; trim away excess clay with a crafts knife. To make a clay border, roll, twist, or cut with decorative-edge scissors. Make a hole for hanging by inserting a toothpick in the clay. Bake again according to product directions. Let cool.

6 Tie on a ribbon to hang the ornament.

CLAY CHRISTMAS ORNAMENTS PATTERN

Crazy quilt trees, stockings, and hearts give a country twist to these ornaments. Hang these holiday creations individually or string them together in a garland to hang from a mantel or stairway railing. See the patterns on pages 68–69.

supplies

Tracing paper; pencil
Scissors; pins
Felt in several colors
Fabric glue
Embroidery floss in colors to contrast with the felt; needle
Assorted holiday buttons and charms, including 2 star buttons
Three 8-inch lengths of ¼-inch ribbon
Fiberfill

what to do

1 Trace and cut out the patterns from *pages 68–69*. Pin the patterns to desired felt colors. Cut out the quilt shapes and two background pieces.

2 Arrange and glue quilt pieces on a background shape, edges together.

3 Use three plies of embroidery floss in contrasting colors to herringbone-stitch over the seams (see diagram, *page 69*). Sew running stitches around the edges.

4 Using the photograph, *opposite,* for placement ideas, sew on buttons (except the star buttons) and charms.

5 Pin the pieced unit on the remaining background shape. Fold a ribbon in half; sandwich the ends between the background shapes, at the top of the tree and at the top heel side of the stocking.

6 Stitch the background edges together using blanket stitches, stopping stitches 2 inches from the beginning stitch. Stuff the ornament with fiberfill; blanket-stitch the opening closed.

7 Sew a star button to each ornament, sewing through the ribbon at the top of the ornament.

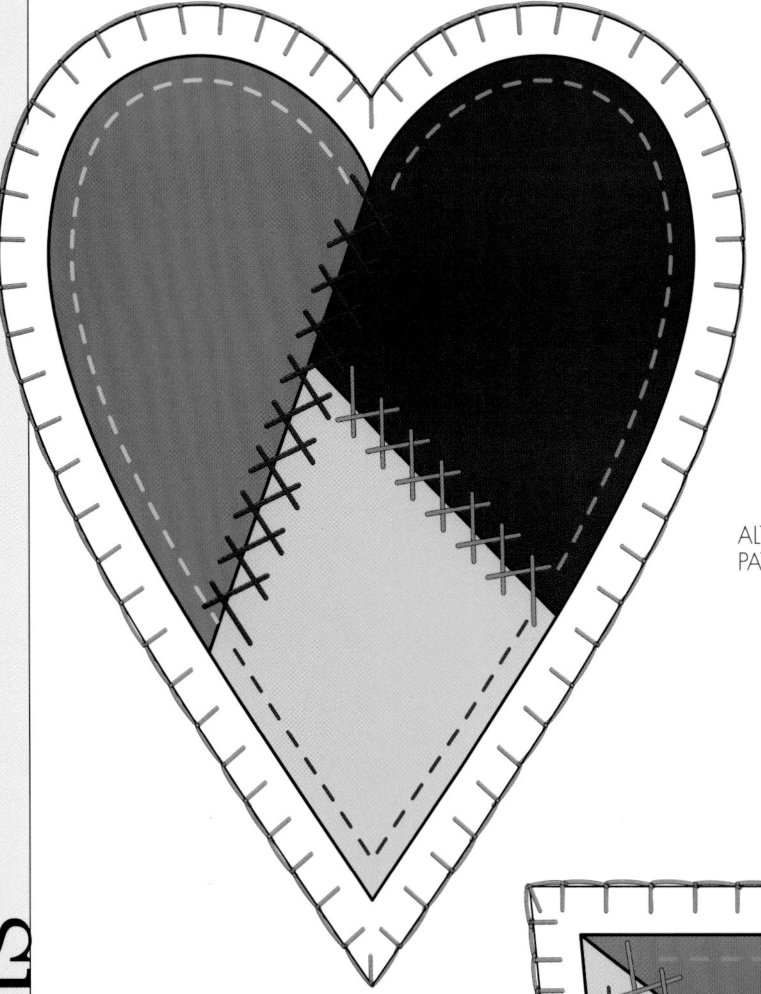

ALTERNATIVE TRIM
PATTERN

OLD-FASHIONED
TRIMS PATTERN

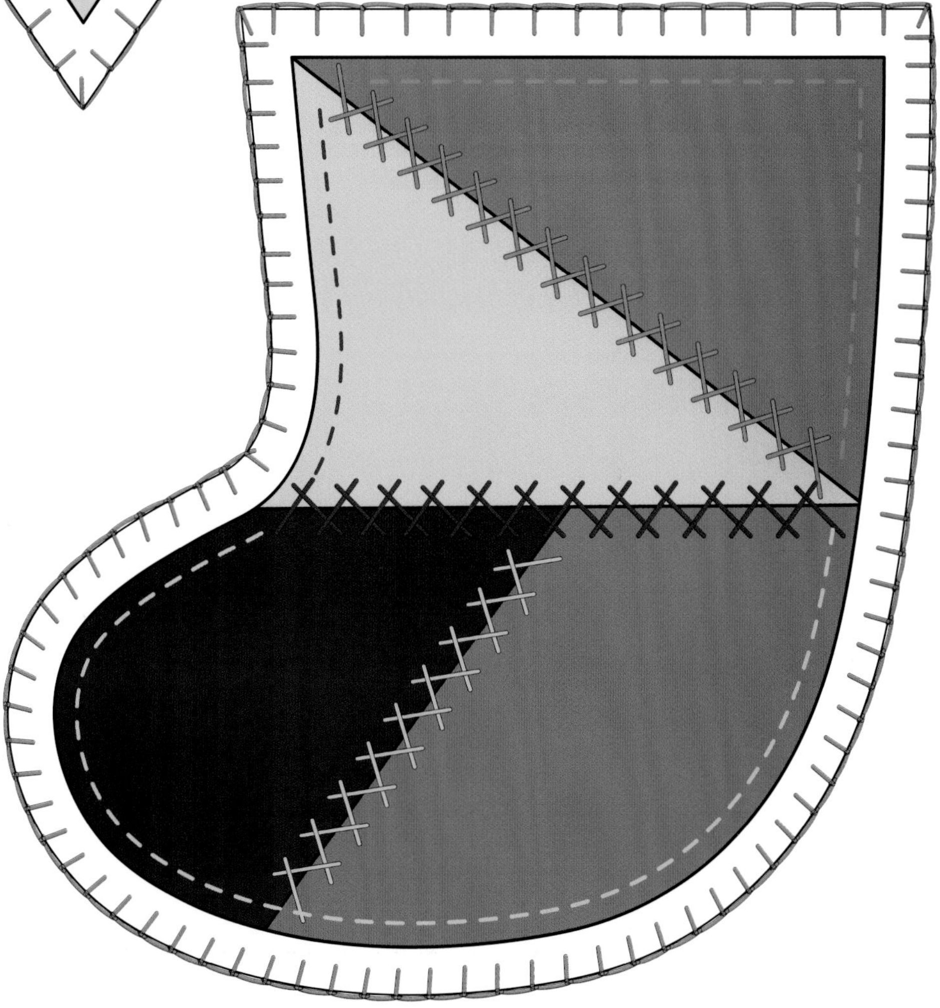

trims patterns

68

BLANKET STITCH

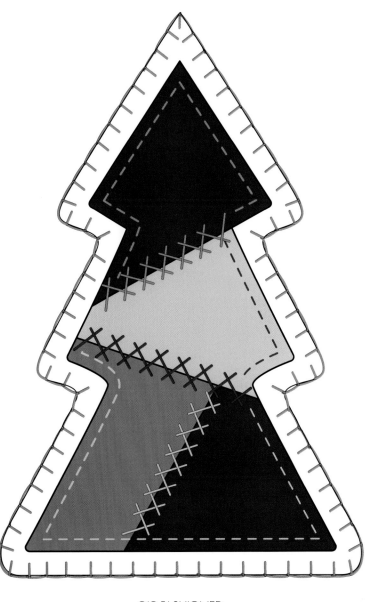

OLD-FASHIONED
TRIMS PATTERN

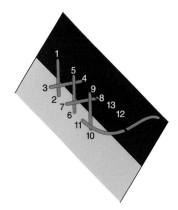

HERRINGBONE STITCH

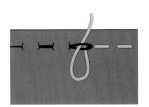

RUNNING STITCH

north woods pillow

Make pillows that fit right into a rustic cabin decor. Single out one from several majestic woodland creature patterns, pages 72–75, to assemble these no-sew projects quickly.

supplies

Square pillow form
Ruler
Fleece in black and red
Fabric marking pencil
Scissors
Tracing paper; pencil
Black suede
Plain terry cloth towel
Ironing board
Double-sided iron-on
  interfacing, such as
  Wonder-Under; iron
Wide black cording

what to do

1 Add 10 inches to the pillow measurements. From the red and black fleece, cut two front pieces and two back pieces to this measurement. Cut a 4-inch square from each corner.

2 Trace and cut out a pattern, *pages 72–75.* Trace around the pattern

continued on page 72

on the right side of the black suede.

3 Lay a plain terry cloth towel on an ironing board (woven designs in textured terry cloth will transfer to the suede during pressing). Center the design on the black suede face down on the towel. Paper side up, layer iron-on interfacing on the suede. Press with a hot, dry iron. Allow the fabric to cool; remove the paper backing. Cut out the design from the suede.

4 Center the design faceup on a piece of red fleece. Dampen a terry cloth towel, lay it on the design, and use a hot iron to fuse the layers. Rather than sliding, lift the iron up, press, and lift again.

5 Align the two red fleece squares together and the two black fleece squares together. Draw a pencil line 5 inches from the outer edges on each set. On the red squares, mark pencil lines ½ inch long and ½ inch apart along the line; cut slits through both fleece layers to insert the

black cording. Weave cording through the slits all around the pillow.

6 Cut 4-inch-long fringes through both layers of red and black fleece, cutting toward the drawn line or the cording.

7 Layer the pillow top front and back pieces, right sides out. Tie three sides of the red fringes and black fringes together to form the pillow cover; insert the pillow form and tie the remaining fringes together to close the opening.

ALTERNATIVE PILLOW PATTERN

NORTH WOODS PILLOW
PATTERN

ALTERNATIVE PILLOW
PATTERNS

GEESE PLACEMENT

ALTERNATIVE PILLOW
PATTERNS

mini tree skirt

Dress up a mini tree for the Christmas season in a colorful skirt. Find the perfect motifs on pages 78–79 to accessorize your holiday decor.

supplies

¼ yard felt in black, blue, red, and yellow; thread; sewing needle; pencil Scissors; rickrack; pinking shears or decorative-edge scissors; tracing paper; ribbon; glue; assorted felt

what to do

1 Use the diagram, *page 79*, to draw two triangles on each felt color; add ¼-inch seam allowance to the sides of each triangle and cut out. Sew the triangles together to form the skirt, overlapping the edges and leaving an opening between two triangles. Topstitch the seams open; trim exposed seams with pinking shears or decorative-edge scissors.

2 Trace and cut out full-size skirt collar pattern, *page 79*. Trace pattern to felt; cut out. Position collar on skirt;

continued on page 78

---

try these ideas

4 *more ways to use these mini tree skirt patterns:*

- *Use the snowflake pattern to make snowflakes from card stock. Punch a hole in the top and hang with string to create a wonderland.*
- *Cut two of one of the stocking patterns from scrapbook paper. Glue the edges, leaving the top open. Use this stocking envelope for giving money at Christmastime.*
- *Stencil the gingerbread man on an apron for fun Christmastime attire.*
- *Use the snowflakes as stencils to paint white snowflakes on a purchased dark tablecloth.*

topstitch in place, leaving an opening at open side of skirt. Pink stitched edges.

3 Insert ribbon ties through the opening of the collar; topstitch in place. Pink the outer edge of the skirt. Mark the wavy border line around the skirt and glue or stitch rickrack in place.

4 Trace and cut out snowflakes or other motifs. Glue or stitch on the motifs. Glue sequins on the skirt. Let the glue dry.

MINI TREE SKIRT
PATTERNS

ALTERNATIVE TREE
SKIRT PATTERNS

ALTERNATIVE TREE SKIRT
PATTERNS

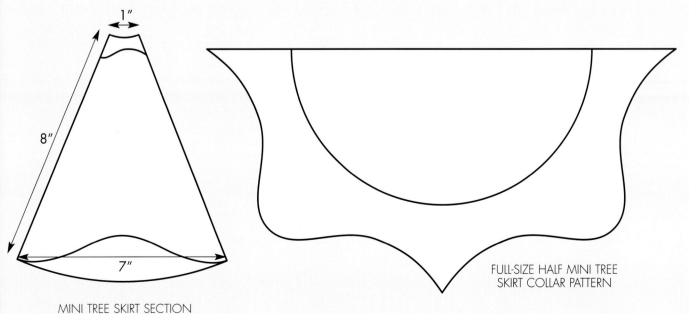

1"

8"

7"

MINI TREE SKIRT SECTION
AND RICKRACK PLACEMENT
DIAGRAM

FULL-SIZE HALF MINI TREE
SKIRT COLLAR PATTERN

Santa's singing, grinning, and yawning team is here to cheer a holiday table—from breakfast through midnight snack.

supplies

Very firm pear
Knife; paintbrush
Place mats; napkins
Tracing paper and pencil
Dark chalk
Acrylic paint in red and tan
Black paint pen
Bronze tube-style fabric paint
Green felt; scissors
Fabric glue
Needle and thread
Jingle bells
Wood napkin rings

what to do

1 Slice a very firm pear cleanly in half.

2 For reindeer faces, brush a generous amount of tan paint on the pear half. Practice stamping it on paper, applying more or less paint to achieve the desired effect. Stamp the pear on place mats and napkins. Let dry.

3 Use the patterns, *opposite*, or draw

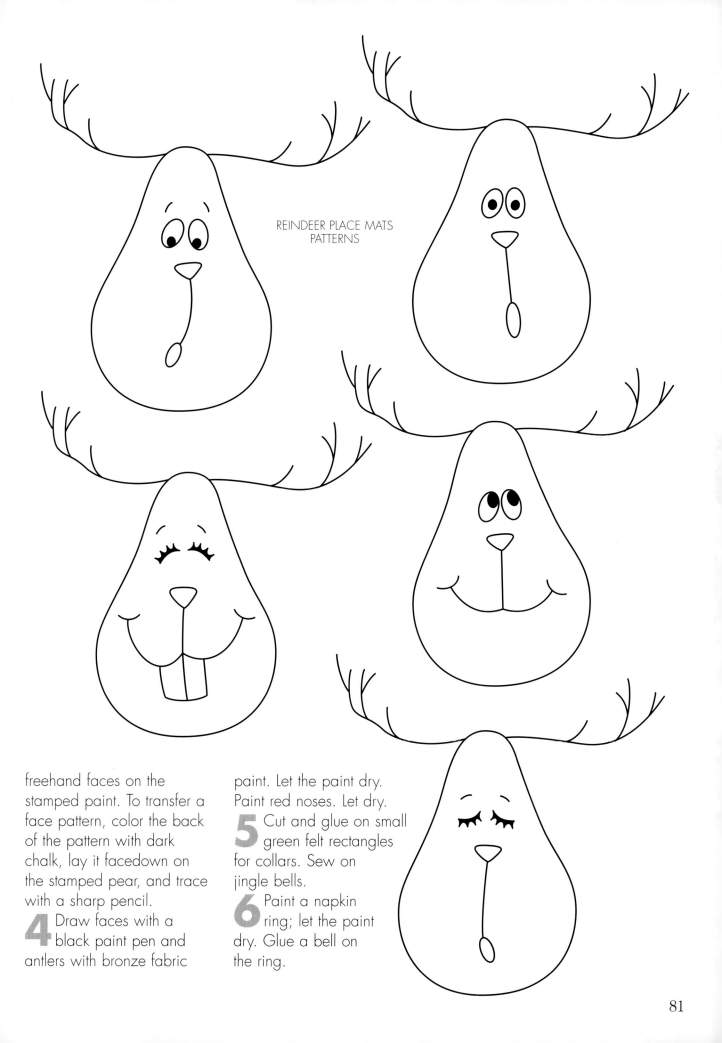

REINDEER PLACE MATS
PATTERNS

freehand faces on the
stamped paint. To transfer a
face pattern, color the back
of the pattern with dark
chalk, lay it facedown on
the stamped pear, and trace
with a sharp pencil.

4 Draw faces with a
black paint pen and
antlers with bronze fabric

paint. Let the paint dry.
Paint red noses. Let dry.

5 Cut and glue on small
green felt rectangles
for collars. Sew on
jingle bells.

6 Paint a napkin
ring; let the paint
dry. Glue a bell on
the ring.

81

hearts

Hearts make a house a home filled with love. This chapter is filled with a variety of heart shapes and clever ways to use them. Take couscous from the pantry to make a beautiful heart box, get out paints and brushes to create a mailbox that

neighbors will admire, or put your paper
scraps to work crafting endearing
valentines. All this and more awaits in
these pages that are bursting with projects
and pattern after pattern from the heart.

A gift in itself or tiny treasure chest, this lovely box is rich with color, texture, and sentiment. Find your favorite hearts, pages 86–89, to make for your sweethearts.

supplies

*Cardboard box with lid
Pencil; tracing paper
Scissors; tape
Narrow cording; couscous
Thick white crafts glue
Acrylic paints in white and
 other desired color
Paintbrush; gold highlighting
 medium, such as Rub 'n' Buff*

what to do

1 Place the lid on the box. Draw a pencil line where the lid meets the box. Remove the lid.

2 Trace a pattern, *pages 86–89*. Darkly pencil the back of the pattern. Trim pattern close to outer edges. Tape the pattern right side up on the lid; retrace the lines (see Photo A, *above right*). Remove the pattern.

3 Cut cording to fit vertically along box bottom to the drawn lid line (see photo, *opposite*). Glue cording sections approximately 1½ inches apart. Cut and glue cording to cover traced lines on box lid (see Photo B). Let the glue dry.

4 Generously apply glue for couscous. Sprinkle couscous onto glue (see Photo C); let the glue dry. Paint the box and lid. Paint the couscous white; let the paint dry.

5 Use your finger to apply highlighting medium on the cording.

A

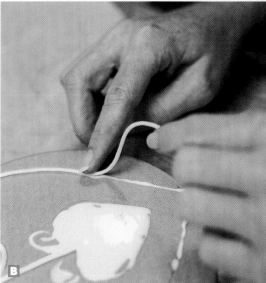

B

C

ELEGANT
HEART BOX
PATTERN

patterns

try these ideas

7 *more ways to use the box patterns:*
- *Appliqué a fabric heart on a quilt block.*
- *Paint the designs on T-shirts.*
- *Cut scrapbook papers to make a valentine.*
- *Paint them on wood or glass circles to make ornaments.*
- *Cut the designs from paper or fabric to decoupage a box lid.*
- *Paint the designs on an album cover.*
- *Make a paper cover for a personalized Valentine's Day coupon book.*

ALTERNATIVE
BOX PATTERN AND
COLOR GUIDES

I Love You

ALTERNATIVE BOX
PATTERN AND
COLOR GUIDE

lovely letter box

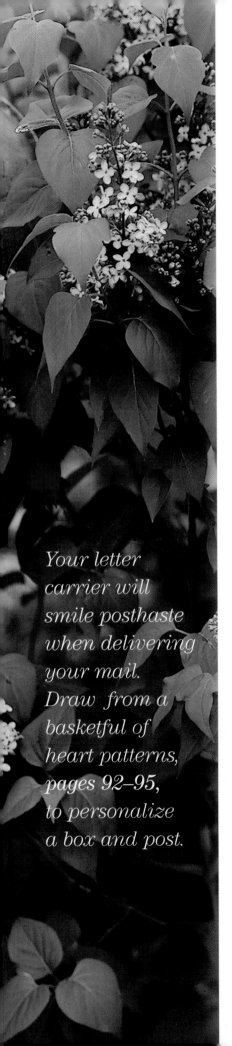

Your letter carrier will smile posthaste when delivering your mail. Draw from a basketful of heart patterns, pages 92–95, to personalize a box and post.

supplies

Newspapers
Metal mailbox
Tools for assembly
White spray primer
Acrylic paints in orange, pale butter yellow, pink, and purple
Disposable plate
Sponge; water
Tracing paper; pencil; scissors
Gold marking pen
2 wood hearts
Paintbrush
Strong adhesive, such as E6000
Spray acrylic sealer
Post

what to do

1 Cover a work surface in a well-ventilated area with newspapers. Evenly spray the mailbox parts with white spray primer, even if they have a coat of white primer already. Let the paint dry. Spray a second coat if needed and let dry.

2 Place quarter-size amounts of paint on a plate. Soak a sponge in water, squeeze out excess, and dab sponge into the paint. Using all of the paint colors, dab different areas of the sponge in paints and then dab the sponge on the inside and outside of the mailbox and flag assembly (see Photo A, *below*), gently blending the colors. Let the paint dry.

continued on page 92

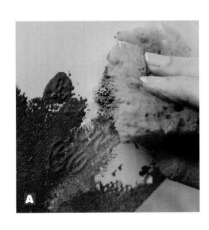

A

3 Trace and cut out heart patterns, *right* and *pages 93–95.* Trace the patterns to the mailbox randomly. Outline the hearts with a gold marking pen (see Photo B, *above).* Fill in the hearts with stripes, swirls, plaid, and other patterns. Let the paint dry.

4 Assemble the mailbox. If the mailbox has a plastic flag, cut the flag from the stem with sharp scissors. Paint two wood hearts purple. Let the paint dry. Detail the hearts with gold marking pen. Glue the hearts to the flag stem. In a well-ventilated work area, spray the mailbox with sealer. Let the sealer dry.

5 Mount the mailbox to a post. If desired, paint the post to coordinate with the mailbox.

LOVELY LETTER BOX
PATTERNS

LOVELY LETTER BOX
PATTERNS

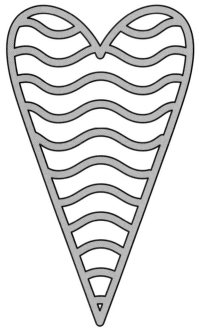

try these ideas

5 *more ways to use the letter box patterns:*

- *Use paint tubes to trace hearts on note cards, T-shirts, or sweatshirts.*
- *Use glue to trace hearts on paper; sprinkle glitter on the wet glue. Mount on card stock for shimmering valentines.*
- *Trace horizontally positioned hearts for ornamental butterfly wings.*
- *Copy hearts on white paper for kids to color and use as gift tags.*
- *Use glass paints to make heart motifs on tiles.*

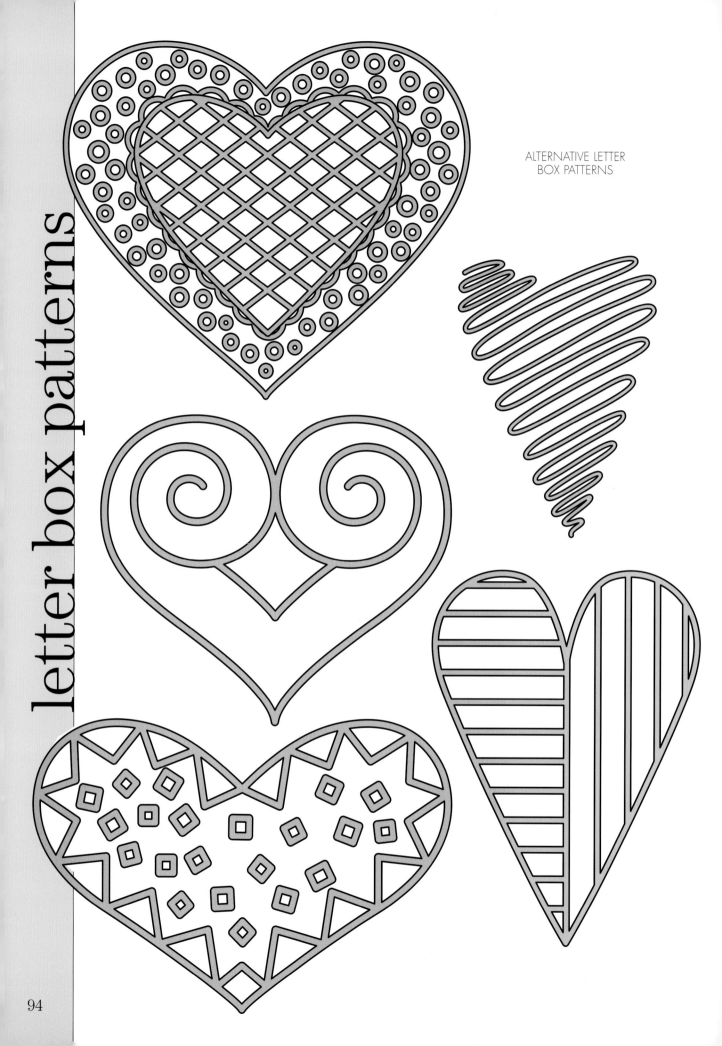

letter box patterns

ALTERNATIVE LETTER
BOX PATTERNS

94

ALTERNATIVE LETTER BOX
PATTERNS

Everyone needs extra tables here and there, so these bright furnishings won't be in the corner for long. Arrange the patterns, pages 98–101, in any order and on any size tabletop.

supplies

Small wood tables with
  finished detachable legs
Plastic; newspapers
White spray primer, such as Kilz
Tracing paper; pencil; scissors
Tape; acrylic paints in hot
  pink, lavender, lime green,
  orange, and yellow

Paintbrushes in medium flat
  and medium round
Medium-point black paint pen
Small and medium
  wood hearts
Wood glue
Beading wire or thread
Black seed beads

what to do

1 Using the patterns, *pages 98–101*, adapt a design to fit a square, round, rectangular, or triangular tabletop. Remove or wrap the table legs with plastic. In a well-ventilated work area, cover work surface with newspapers. Spray primer on the tabletop; let the primer dry.

2 Enlarge and trace the patterns to tracing paper. Cut out a wavy line pattern, using the placement diagram, *page 101*, as a guide. Centering the curved borders, tape the patterns to the table edges.

3 **For the bird table,** paint the center section hot pink, the border orange, and the edge lime green. Let the paint dry. Apply a second coat if necessary; let the paint dry.

4 Transfer the birds to the pink area. Paint the birds yellow, lime green, orange, and lavender. Let the paint dry.

5 Use a medium-point black paint pen to draw hearts randomly on the tabletop. Let the ink dry. Fill in the hearts with lavender, lime green, and yellow paint. Apply dots and dashes as shown on the patterns. To apply dots, dip a paintbrush handle in paint and dot the tabletop.

6 Outline the birds and draw stripes on the table edge with paint pen.

7 **For the heart table,** paint the top yellow and the edges pink. Transfer heart patterns. Paint and detail as for the bird table.

8 Paint wood hearts as shown on patterns. Use wood glue to join two hearts. String beads on beading wire or thread, leaving at least 3 inches on each end. Glue one end to heart back and other under tabletop. Reassemble table if necessary.

FOLK ART TABLES PATTERN

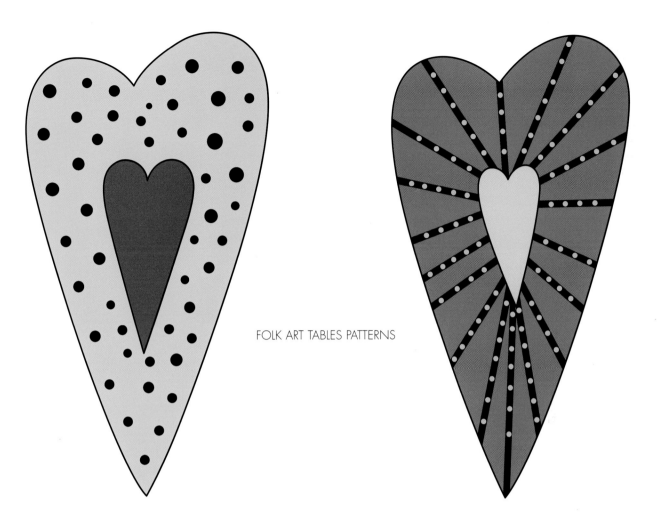

FOLK ART TABLES PATTERNS

11 *more ways to use the table patterns:*

- *Cut out a heart pattern from a thick piece of wood. Paint it and drill a hole in the center to make a candleholder.*
- *Transfer the heart patterns to colored paper for valentines.*
- *Cut out the heart patterns from colored card stock. Place a photo in the center for someone special.*
- *Use the patterns to make felt ornaments for Christmas, adjusting the colors to suit your decorating tastes.*
- *Enlarge the desired heart pattern to make a felt pillow.*
- *Add a heart-shape pocket to a plain T-shirt or sweatshirt.*
- *Use the heart outlines as guides to shape clay ornaments, paper weights, and coasters.*
- *Use the bird patterns, pages 100–101, to make a cut-paper border for any room.*
- *Cut out the patterns from decorative papers to add whimsy to scrapbook pages.*
- *Appliqué a parade of birds across the edge of a quilt.*
- *Appliqué a large heart on background fabric, and embellish with decorative stitches to make a striking wall hanging.*

FOLK ART TABLES PATTERNS

FOLK ART TABLES
PLACEMENT
DIAGRAM

FOLK ART TABLES PATTERN

Take advantage of the plethora of heart shapes, pages 104–105, that are perfect for your Valentine verses. Stitched or glued, these heart-throbs are bound to spell love.

trio-of-hearts card

supplies

*7¾x7½-inch rectangle purple
  card stock*
*7¼x3¼-inch rectangle red
  card stock*
Glue stick
*7x3-inch rectangle
  purple-and-white patterned
  scrapbook paper*
*Three 4-inch squares red card
  stock*
*Sewing machine; white
  sewing thread*
Tracing paper; pencil; scissors
Scrap of purple card stock

what to do

1 Fold the purple card
stock in half to measure
7¾x3¾ inches. Center and
mount the red card stock
rectangle on the card front;
layer patterned scrapbook
paper on the red.

2 Machine-stitch straight,
zigzag, or other stitch
designs on each of the red
card stock squares.

3 Trace and cut out heart
patterns, *pages
104–105.* Trace a heart on
the back of each stitched
square; cut out the hearts.

4 Glue each stitched
heart to a scrap of
purple card stock; trim
⅛ inch beyond the
stitched hearts.

5 Space the hearts
evenly across the card
front and glue in place.

ribbon heart card

supplies

*6x12-inch rectangle bright
  orange card stock*
*5⅞-inch square patterned
  vellum; glue stick*
*5-inch square pink-and-white
  polka-dot paper*
*4-inch squares bright orange
  and purple card stock*
Card stock in red and pink
Sewing machine; white thread
*Trims, such as ribbons and
  plastic string*
Tracing paper; pencil; scissors

what to do

1 Fold the bright orange
card stock in half for a
6-inch square. Center and
glue the center of the vellum
to the card front. Center and
mount the polka-dot paper
on the vellum. Center and
mount the bright orange
square on the polka-dot
paper. Center the purple
square like a diamond and
mount on the orange square.

2 Machine-stitch trims on
a piece of pink card
stock large enough to fit a
heart, *pages 104–105.*

3 Trace and cut out a
heart pattern; trace on
the back of the embellished
card stock; cut out. Mount
the heart on red card stock;
trim a border beyond the
embellished pink heart.

4 Center and mount the
layered heart on the
purple diamond.

HAVE-A-HEART
VALENTINES PATTERNS

silky sachets

Make enchanting sachets from painted silk in a rainbow of colors, accented with rub-off foil and edged with fringes. Choose fanciful heart patterns from pages 108–10, to make a drawer full of elegance.

supplies

¾ cup rice
Plastic sandwich bag with tight
closure; scented oil
Sheet of white paper
Two 6-inch squares of
medium-weight white silk
Scissors; spray bottle of water
Acrylic paints in blue, copper,
green, and magenta
Disposable plate
Paintbrush; iron; pencil
Kit of gold rub-off foil,
adhesive, and sealer
28 inches of gold fringe
Straight pins; sewing machine
Funnel; needle and thread

what to do

1 Place rice in a plastic bag; add four drops of scented oil (see Photo A, *right*). Shake well, seal, and let set for at least one hour.

2 Place white paper on a flat work surface. Smooth the silk squares on the paper. Spray the silk with water until thoroughly wet but not dripping (see Photo B).

3 Place small amounts of paint on a plate; thin with water if needed until paint is consistency of light cream. Dip the brush in paint and brush onto wet silk. Wash the paintbrush between each color and apply different colors to the silk (see Photo C). Brush the paints together, covering all silk surfaces and allowing

continued on page 108

A

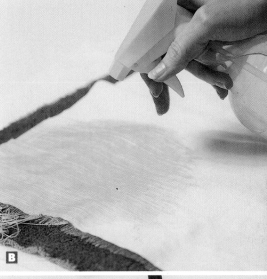

B

C

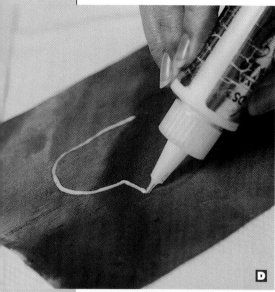

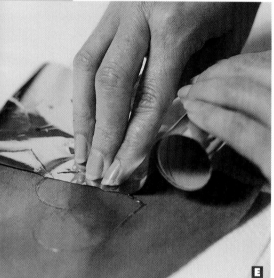

D

E

paints to bleed together. Let the paints dry.

4 To apply rub-off foil hearts, use a pencil and any of the patterns, *below* and *opposite*, to draw or trace hearts at least 1¼ inches from the fabric edge. Trace over the pencil line with the foil adhesive (see Photo D). The adhesive will appear milky as it is applied and will dry clear. The adhesive should be tacky, yet firm enough not to smear.

5 Right side up, place the gold foil sheet on the adhesive (see Photo E). Rub gently with your fingertips to adhere the gold foil to the adhesive. Pull away excess foil. Seal the gold foil with the clear sealer included with the foil.

6 Lay one embellished silk square right side up. Pin gold fringe along the edge, raw edges together. Sew the fringe close to the edge of the square.

7 Right sides facing, pin a second silk square on the trimmed square. Sew the pieces together using a ½-inch seam allowance and leaving a 1½-inch opening along one side for turning and filling.

8 Turn the silk to the right side. Use a funnel to fill the sachet bag with the scented rice. Hand-sew the opening closed.

patterns

SILKY SACHETS PATTERNS

ALTERNATIVE SACHET PATTERNS

babies and children

Brighten up a child's day by making your favorite little boy or girl something to wear—or something to jazz up his or her room! This animated chapter offers ideas for cute birthday shirts, adorable window

dressings, precious scrapbook covers, and other creative projects that make kids grin with delight. From cupcakes to singing mice, discover just the right theme to put sparkle in your little someone's eyes.

it's your day t-shirt

Everyone knows it's a special day when a child wears this special birthday shirt. Choose from the cheerful patterns on pages 114–115.

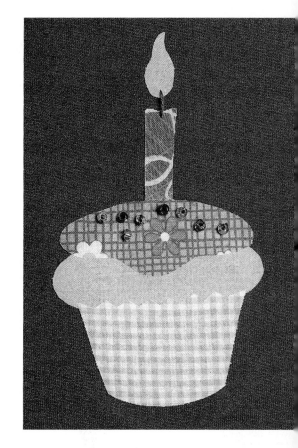

supplies

Tracing paper; pencil; scissors
Bright patterned fabric scraps
Fusible fabric adhesive, such
* as Heat 'n' Bond; iron*
Prewashed T-shirt in bright color
Embroidery floss in blue, pink,
* purple, and yellow*
Glass beads in bright colors
Sewing needle

what to do

1 Trace and cut out your choice of objects, *pages 114–115*. Coordinate the fabrics for the designs.

2 Fuse fabric adhesive to the wrong side of the fabrics, keeping the paper backing intact. Trace the shapes to the paper side of the fusible adhesive. Cut out the shapes.

3 Peel off the paper backing; arrange and layer the fabric pieces on the T-shirt. When satisfied with the arrangement, use a hot, dry iron to fuse the fabrics to the shirt one fabric at a time.

4 Embellish the shirt designs by stitching bead "sprinkles" on the cupcake icing, an embroidery floss wick on the candle, and floss strings on the balloons.

---

try these ideas

4 more ways to use the T-shirt patterns:

- *Transfer the patterns to a party tablecloth. Let the birthday party guests color on the tablecloth with permanent markers.*
- *Transfer the desired motifs to white paper and color the shapes with colored pencil or marking pens. Reduce the patterns and use on the front of the birthday invitations.*
- *Cut the shapes of the patterns from scrapbook papers. Reassemble the patterns on a scrapbook page complete with pictures of the party.*
- *Enlarge the desired patterns and cut from fabric. Appliqué the pieces on a fabric flag or banner to announce the party.*

ALTERNATIVE T-SHIRT PATTERNS

IT'S YOUR DAY
T-SHIRT PATTERN

ALTERNATIVE T-SHIRT PATTERNS

Paint just a few of these happy designs from pages 119–123, or confidently combine them all. The pretty pastels and comical designs cheer and inspire anyone who sits at this adorable set.

supplies

Table and chair
Sandpaper; tack cloth
White spray primer, such as Kilz
Acrylic paints in cream
  and pastels
Paintbrushes: 2-inch flat, stencil
  brush, small round, medium
  round, flat, and liner
Photocopier; tracing paper
Pencil (with sharp hard lead)
Stencil acetate; tape
Crafts knife; rubber cement
Disposable plate
Paper; paper towels
Transfer paper
Needle-tip paint bottle
  for outlining
Glitter paint in bottle
Heavy-gloss glaze sealer
Casting resin
Disposable glass or metal
  container for mixing
Newspapers; crafts stick

what to do

1 Begin with a clean, dry table and chair. Sand any rough spots. Wipe off dust with a tack cloth.

2 Apply one or two coats of spray primer, allowing ample drying time for each coat.

3 Base-coat the table and chair with two coats of cream acrylic paint, using the 2-inch flat brush and allowing drying time for each coat.

4 Photocopy or trace the patterns, *pages 119–123.* Use the tracings to plan motif placement on the tabletop and chair. Cut letters, notes, and tiny items from stencil acetate using a

continued on page 118

117

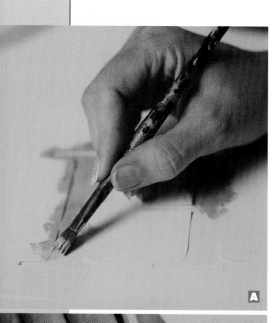

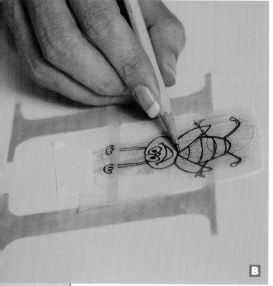

A

B

the almost dry brush and a pouncing or light brushing motion to fill in each letter (see Photo A, *left*), brushing from the outer edge to the inner edge. When the brush is almost dry, reapply a small amount of paint. Keeping the brush nearly dry prevents paint from seeping under the stencil and smearing the design. Stencil each letter a different color. Let the paint dry; remove the stencils.

6 Tape the patterns face up on the painted surfaces, insert transfer paper between the pattern and painted surface, and trace the designs using a sharp hard lead pencil (see Photo B). Remove paper. Paint the motifs using pastel paints and the brush size that best fits each area. Use the liner brush to detail. Let the paint dry.

7 Mix paint and water to the consistency of light cream to outline shapes. Put the paint mixture in the needle-tip paint bottle. Test the paint consistency on paper. Too-thin paint runs; too-thick paint stays in the bottle. Outline the motifs; let the paint dry.

8 Paint the table edges small blocks of color. Paint the chair spindles a variety of colors. Let the paint dry. Apply glitter paint to areas around figures. Let dry.

9 Spray the table and chair legs with gloss glaze sealer. Let the sealer dry.

10 Apply the casting resin to the tabletop and chair seat. In a well-ventilated area, cover a work surface with newspapers. Mix the resin in a disposable container according to product directions. Working with one surface at a time, pour resin on the table or chair; smooth with a crafts stick. Remove drips from the table or chair edges. Let the resin dry thoroughly for several hours or days, depending on humidity. Apply additional coats until the dimensional glitter is level with the surface.

crafts knife (reserve the inner portions of a's and p's).

5 Place small amounts of pastel paints on a plate. Stencil or paint the words and letters first. Firmly tape stencils in place; apply a dab of rubber cement to inner letter portions that were cut out and position them in the stencil. Dab the stencil brush in the paint. Dab off most of the paint on the plate or a paper towel. Use

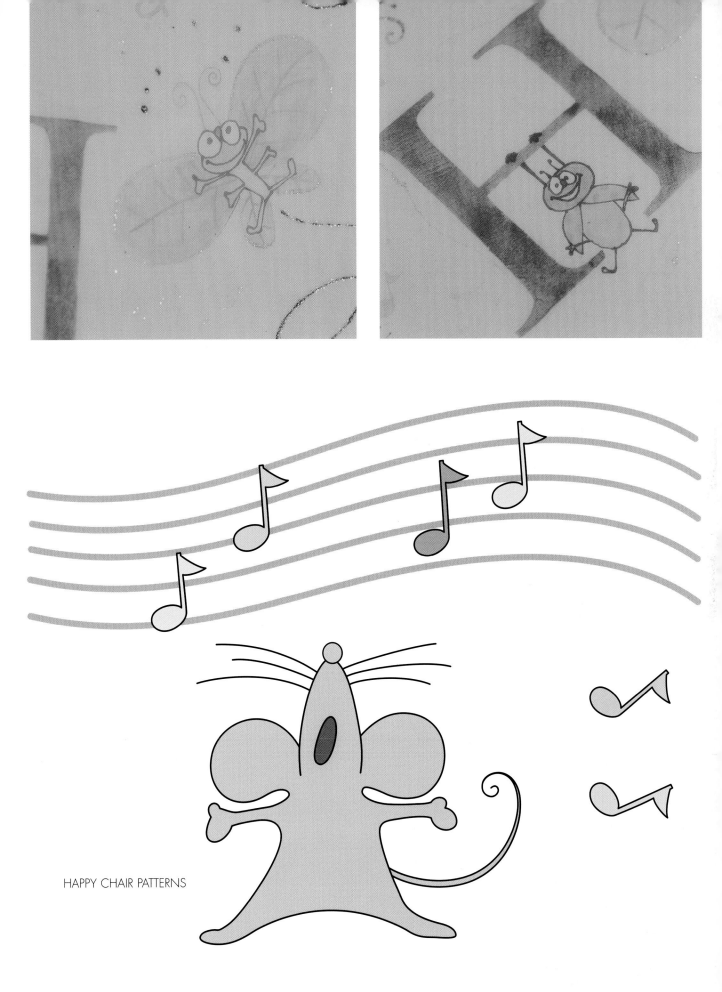

HAPPY CHAIR PATTERNS

HAPPY TABLE AND CHAIR
PATTERNS

HAPPY TABLE AND CHAIR
PATTERNS

121

HAPPY TABLE AND CHAIR
PATTERNS

HAPPY TABLE
PLACEMENT
DIAGRAM

Graphic designs make these paper kites oh-so-fun to put together. Use the patterns, below and pages 126–127, to make the kites that soar with surprises.

supplies

Tracing paper; pencil
Scissors
Paper punch
Crafts knife
Adhesive-back craft foam
Colored papers plus extra
  piece for place cards
Glue stick
Heavy, pliable colored wire
Small glass votive holder
Strong adhesive, such as
  Liquid Nails; tape
Coordinating ribbon; candy
Tube-style fabric paint

what to do

1 Trace and cut out a pattern, *right* through *page 127*. Use a paper punch to make circles.

2 Cut the kite background from adhesive-back foam using scissors or a crafts knife.

3 Carefully layer the paper pieces on the adhesive side of the foam.

4 Cut small paper pieces and attach using a glue stick.

5 Wind a wire kite tail around a votive holder. Use strong adhesive to affix the wire to the back of the kite, temporarily holding the wire in place with tape until the glue sets.

6 Tie small ribbon bows to the kite tail. Fill the glass with candy. Make a paper place card, write a name with fabric paint, and glue the card to a toothpick. Insert the name card in the candy.

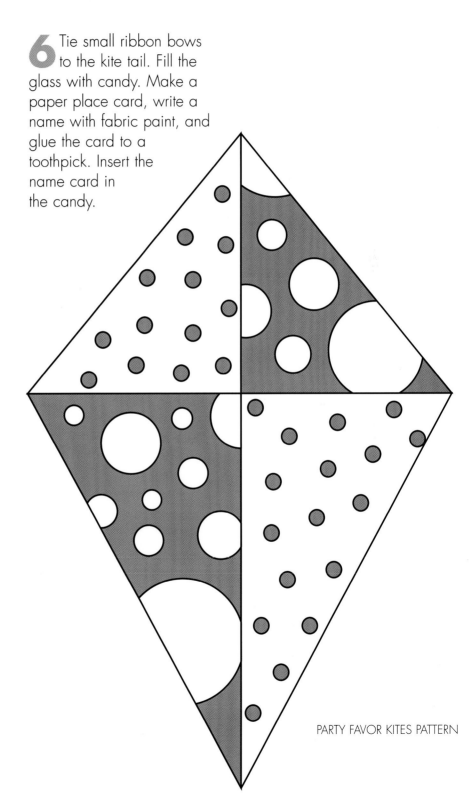

PARTY FAVOR KITES PATTERN

PARTY FAVOR KITES PATTERN

ALTERNATIVE KITE PATTERN

kite patterns

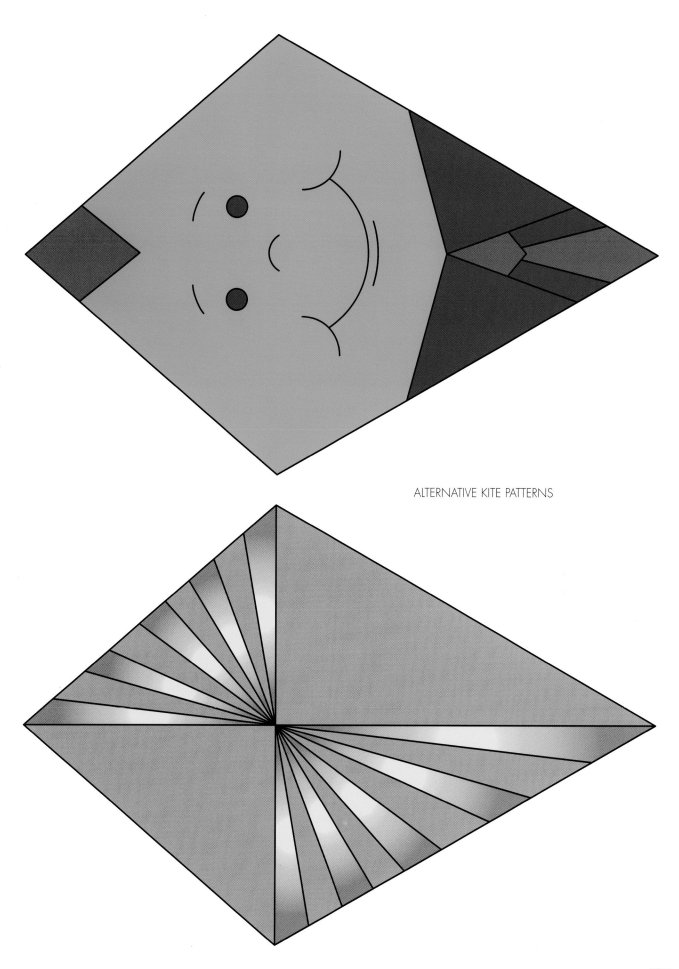

ALTERNATIVE KITE PATTERNS

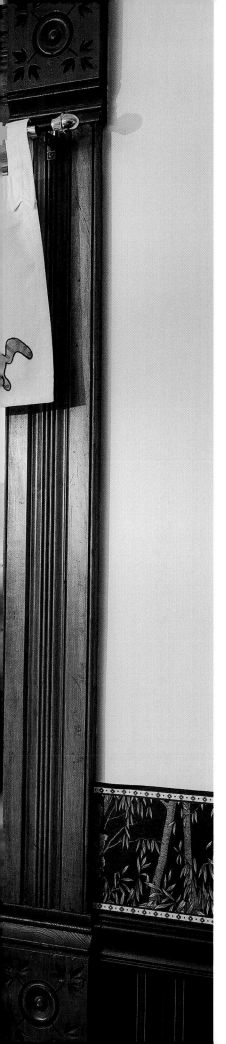

supplies

Photocopier
Tracing paper
Sharp pencil
Black fabric-transfer pen
Iron
Ironing board
Curtains in white or light color
Projector
Primer
Pins
Acrylic paints
Paintbrush
Textile paint medium

what to do

1 Photocopy (same size, enlarged, or reduced) or trace patterns, *pages 130–139.* Trace right side of all design lines with the fabric-transfer pen.

2 Trim patterns close to the designs. Position and pin the patterns facedown on the fabric.

3 Set the iron temperature for the fabric content; test on an inconspicuous portion of the fabric. Secure the drawing firmly in place. Press in a circular motion to transfer the image to the fabric, increasing the iron temperature slightly if necessary. Each drawing

should provide more than one impression (see Photo A, *above*).

continued on page 130

A parade of playful characters on a curtain and valance set entertains youngsters for many years. Pair up a few animals, pages 130-139, or a whole set to fill the ark.

4 Mix one part textile paint medium, two parts paint, and enough water to equal the consistency of light cream. Use a fabric paintbrush to apply paint as shown in Photo B, *page 129.* Let the paint dry. Heat-set the painted designs with an iron.

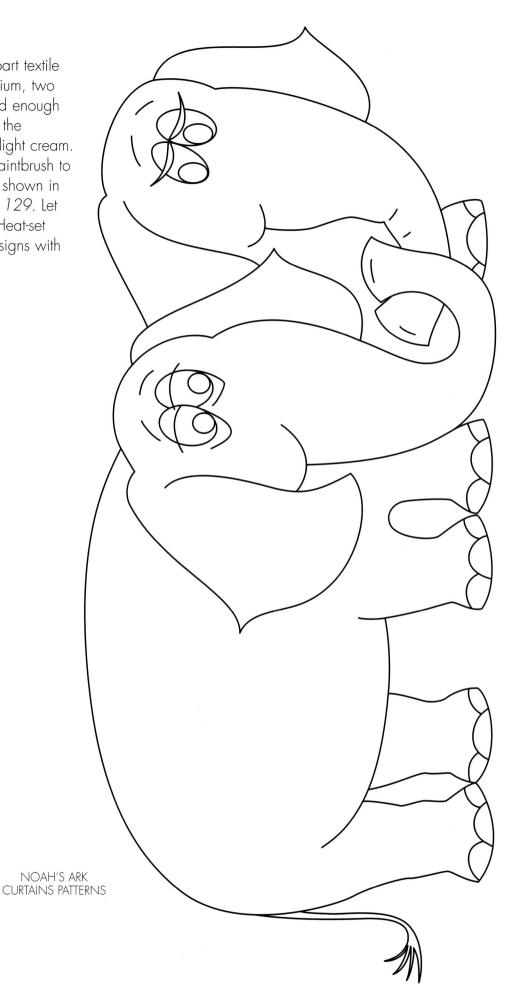

NOAH'S ARK
CURTAINS PATTERNS

NOAH'S ARK
CURTAINS PATTERNS

131

NOAH'S ARK
CURTAINS PATTERNS

ALTERNATIVE CURTAINS
PATTERNS

patterns

NOAH'S ARK
CURTAINS PATTERNS

NOAH'S ARK
CURTAINS PATTERNS

ALTERNATIVE CURTAINS
PATTERNS

7 more ways to use the curtain patterns:

- *Cut all of the pieces from felt to make a cling play board.*
- *Sew dolls from the large character patterns.*
- *Trace and cut out paper animals to adorn kids' birthday cards.*
- *Appliqué the animals on sheets and pillowcases.*
- *Appliqué a bed quilt or wall hanging.*
- *Show kids how to make coloring books by tracing the shapes.*
- *Enlarge designs and transfer to canvas for painting.*

patterns

ALTERNATIVE CURTAINS
PATTERN

NOAH'S ARK
CURTAINS PATTERN

ALTERNATIVE CURTAINS
PATTERNS

137

ALTERNATIVE CURTAINS
PATTERNS

try these ideas

5 _more ways to use the curtain patterns:_

- _Transfer your favorite animal duo to a T-shirt and color in the areas with fabric paint._
- _Enlarge the patterns and trace around them on a child's bedroom door._
- _Enlarge the patterns on a long piece of white butcher paper and let five or six children color in the animals, creating a great mural._
- _Copy the patterns and put them into a small take-along book for your child to color in while in the car._
- _Transfer your favorite pattern to a glass tabletop and paint with glass paints._

ALTERNATIVE CURTAINS
PATTERNS

trinket troves

Here's a project that kids love to make and use—tiny painted boxes with craft foam features. For lots of summer fun ideas, see the patterns on pages 142–143.

supplies

Cardboard box with lid in
  any shape
Acrylic paints in bright pink,
  light blue, light pink, lime
  green, white, yellow, or
  other colors
Paintbrush
Tracing paper
Pencil
Scissors
Craft foam in black, dark
  green, light green, orange,
  yellow, white, or other colors
Thick white crafts glue

what to do

1 Paint the box and lid contrasting colors. Let the paint dry. If desired, paint colorful stripes on the box sides. Let dry.

2 Trace the patterns, *pages 142–143*, onto tracing paper and cut out. Trace the shapes onto craft foam. Cut out the shapes.

3 Layer and glue the foam pieces together. Glue the foam shapes on the box. If desired, paint details, such as sun rays or polka dots. To make small dots, dip a paintbrush handle in paint; touch the handle end to a surface to dot. For large dots, apply paint with a round pencil eraser. Let the paint dry.

TRINKET TROVES
PATTERNS

Cover photo albums for wee ones with
a menagerie of cuddly critters. See the
pattern assortment, pages 146–149,
for even more sweet ideas.

zoo baby album
supplies

Fabric pieces
Fusible fabric adhesive, such
  as Heat 'n' Bond
Tracing paper; pencil; scissors
Thick white crafts glue
Undecorated photo album
Light brown embroidery floss
Tiny pom-poms
1 yard of 1½-inch-wide ribbon

what to do

1 Coordinate fabrics for the giraffe or other animals, *pages 146–149.* Fuse fabric adhesive to the wrong side of the fabrics, leaving the paper intact for tracing the designs.

2 Trace and cut out the selected pattern pieces. Trace the patterns to the paper side of the fusible adhesive on the fabrics. Cut out the shapes. Peel off the paper backing.

3 Use crafts glue to assemble the pieces on the photo album cover. To position animals on clothing, blankets, or fabric bags, use a hot dry iron to press the designs in place.

4 For the giraffe tail, braid strands of embroidery floss. Knot one end; slip the opposite end under the fabric. Glue on pom-poms for eyes and nose. Wrap a wide ribbon around the front of the photo album, tie a bow, and trim the ribbon ends.

zoo baby pillowcase
supplies
Fabrics in assorted prints
Fusible fabric adhesive, such as Heat 'n' Bond; iron
Tracing paper; pencil; scissors
Light brown embroidery floss
Plain pillowcase

what to do

1 Coordinate fabrics for the animal patterns, *pages 146–149.* Apply fusible adhesive to the wrong side of the fabrics, leaving the paper intact.

2 Trace and cut out the patterns. Trace the patterns to the paper backing; cut out the fabric shapes on the traced lines. Peel off the paper backing.

3 Fuse the designs to a pillowcase, using photos, *right,* as a guide.

4 For the giraffe tail, braid strands of embroidery floss. Knot one end; slip the opposite end under the fabric. Stitch eye and nose details with embroidery floss.

Appliqué a baby quilt using the zoo animal patterns.

try these ideas

5 *more ways to use the zoo baby patterns:*

- *Appliqué a baby quilt using the zoo animal patterns.*
- *Make a fabric diaper bag and appliqué the animals on the front.*
- *Appliqué a favorite animal on a baby bib.*
- *Trace the shapes onto paper and cut out to make a gift card.*
- *Cut animals from felt to sew on a pillow top.*

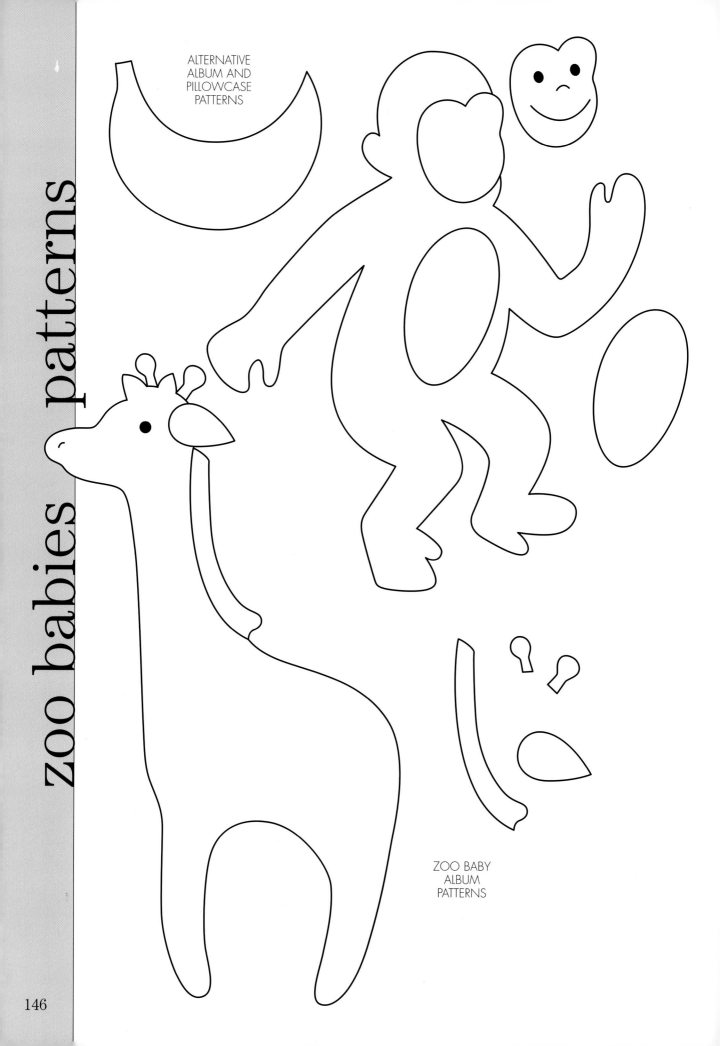

ALTERNATIVE
ALBUM AND
PILLOWCASE
PATTERNS

ZOO BABY
ALBUM
PATTERNS

ALTERNATIVE
ALBUM AND
PILLOWCASE
PATTERNS

try these ideas

8 more ways to use the album and pillowcase patterns:

- *Cut the shapes from craft foam for kids to glue together.*
- *Cut paper animals to decoupage on the lid of a toy box.*
- *Appliqué the desired animals on a fabric-covered headboard.*
- *Cut the shapes from scrapbook papers to enhance the pages of a baby book.*
- *Cut the shapes from felt for children to play with on a felt jungle scene glued to a board.*
- *Enlarge a favorite animal motif and use it to appliqué a fabric animal on a child's bathrobe.*
- *Appliqué several animals on a beach towel for a little one.*
- *Enlarge the motifs to life-size and paint on a child's wall.*

ZOO BABY
PILLOWCASE
PATTERNS

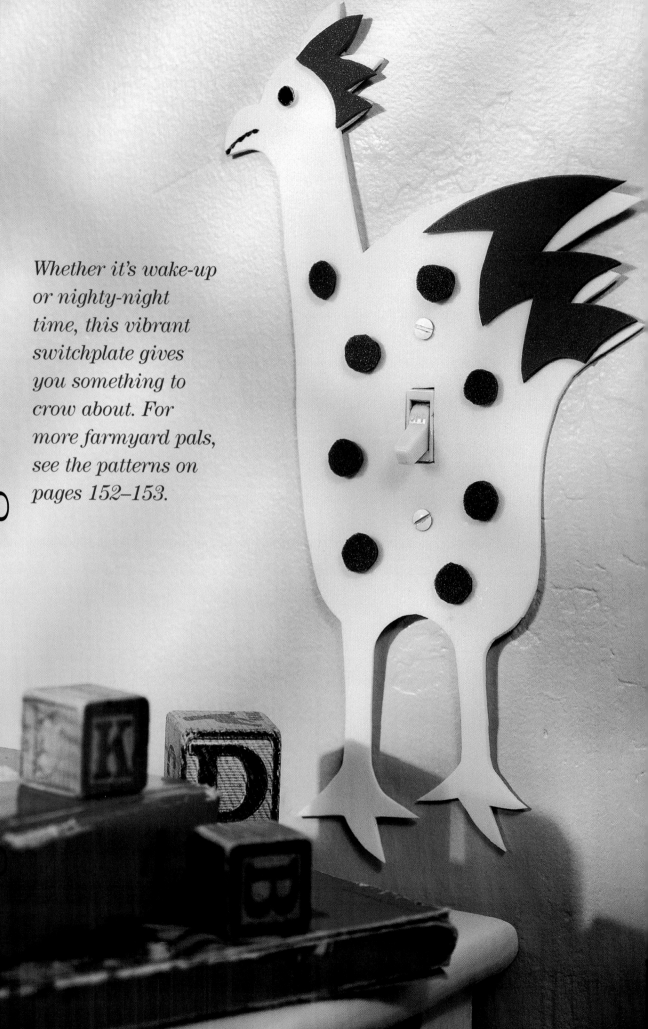

Whether it's wake-up or nighty-night time, this vibrant switchplate gives you something to crow about. For more farmyard pals, see the patterns on pages 152–153.

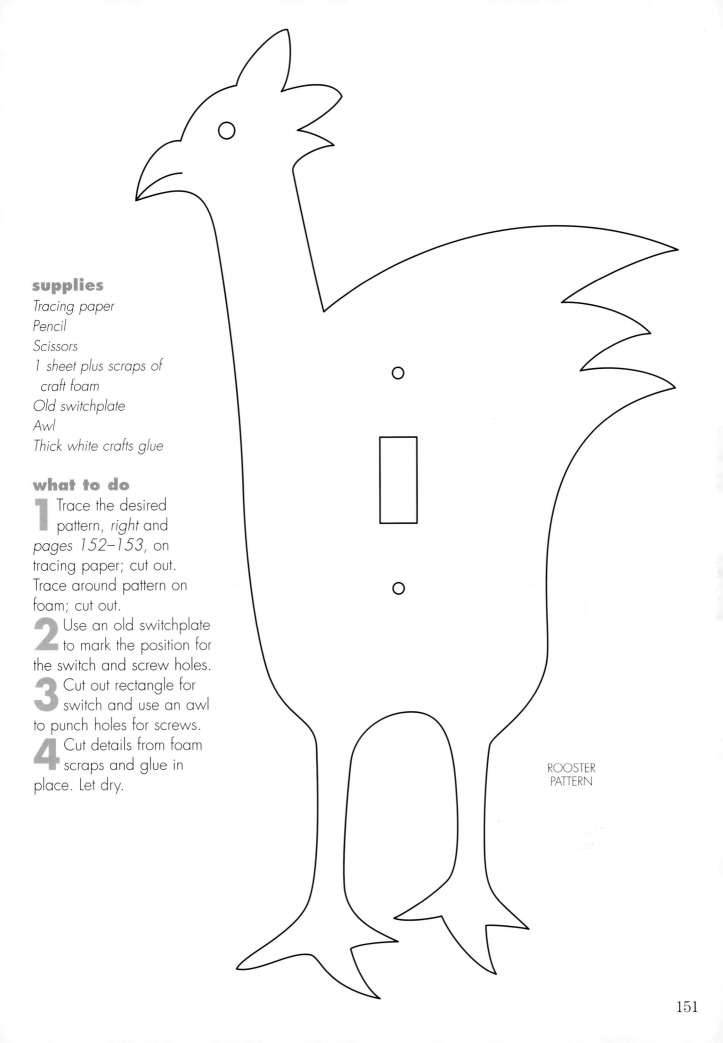

supplies

Tracing paper
Pencil
Scissors
1 sheet plus scraps of
  craft foam
Old switchplate
Awl
Thick white crafts glue

what to do

1 Trace the desired pattern, *right* and pages 152–153, on tracing paper; cut out. Trace around pattern on foam; cut out.

2 Use an old switchplate to mark the position for the switch and screw holes.

3 Cut out rectangle for switch and use an awl to punch holes for screws.

4 Cut details from foam scraps and glue in place. Let dry.

ROOSTER
PATTERN

151

ALTERNATIVE
COW
PATTERN

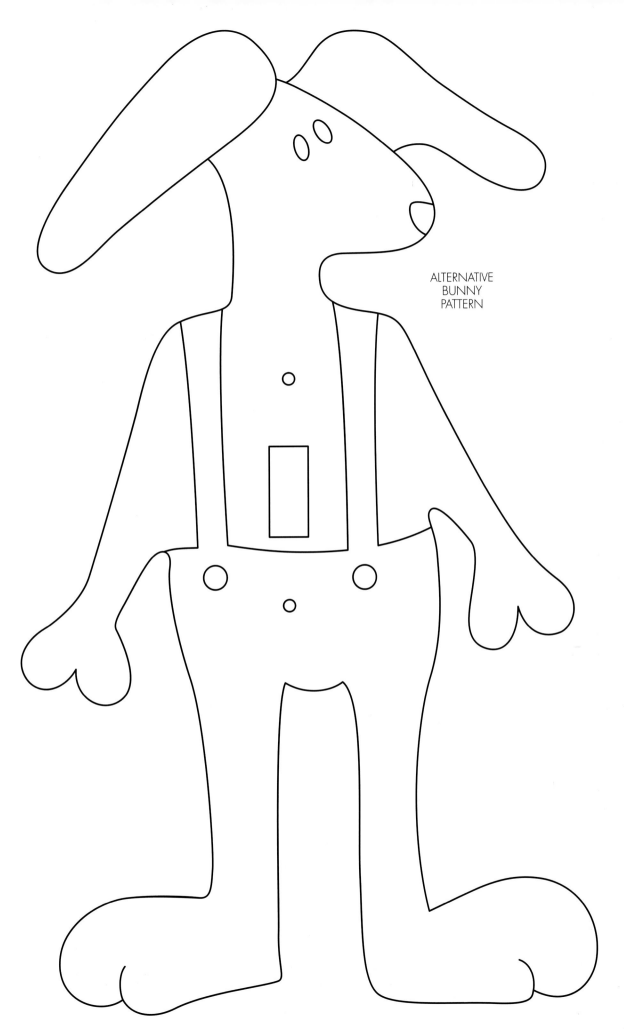

ALTERNATIVE
BUNNY
PATTERN

spring and summer

Get in the swing of warm-weather seasons with delightful fresh-as-a-daisy patterns. Painting, decoupaging, and etching are a few of the many techniques

*explored in this chapter. From Easter eggs
to paper mosaic stools, have a wonderful
time crafting several charming projects.*

Welcome spring with beautifully painted eggs, budding with lilies, jonquils, and other flowers. See the patterns, pages 158–159, for inspiring spring ideas.

supplies

Photocopier
Light box, if desired
Hard lead pencil
Adhesive-back paper,
 such as for labels
Crafts knife
Blown-out real or plaster
 crafts eggs
Stencil paints; stencil brush
Disposable plate

what to do

1 Photocopy patterns, *pages 158–159*. Trace designs to adhesive-back paper using a light box or sunlit window and a hard lead pencil.

2 Carefully cut along the traced lines with a crafts knife (see Photo A, *right*). Remove backing from design; adhere to each egg.

3 Place paint on a disposable plate. Dab stencil brush in the paint, dab off most of the paint, and apply sparingly with a pouncing motion to fill in the open area of the design (see Photo B). Let the paint dry.

4 When necessary, cut away portions of the stencil as you paint, setting pieces aside to reuse as needed. Continue painting in designs (see Photo C).

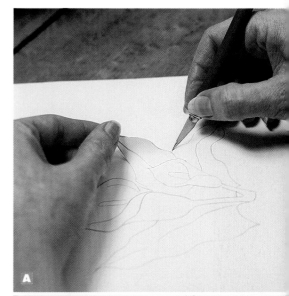

STENCILED EGGS PATTERN

try these ideas

10 *more ways to use the egg patterns:*

- *Transfer and paint designs on a pail or a new gallon paint can to use for an egg hunt.*
- *Use fabric paint to draw a floral illustration on a felt Easter bonnet.*
- *Paint the flowers on a table runner.*
- *Use paint markers and a motif to embellish a fabric tote bag.*
- *Cut the daffodil design from paper and decoupage it on a hat box.*
- *Appliqué the lily pattern to fabric for a pillow top.*
- *Paint any flower on a plain note card.*
- *Paint the circular floral design,* opposite, *on a round box lid.*
- *Use a wood-burning tool to transfer designs to a wood plate, box, or small tabletop.*
- *Use glass paints to make a set of floral tumblers, creating a different design on each glass.*

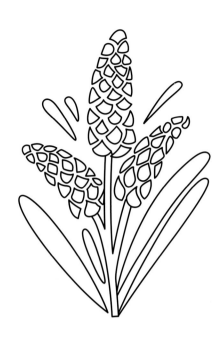

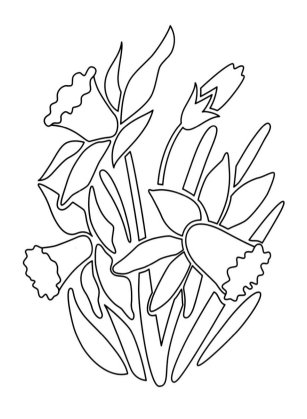

STENCILED EGGS PATTERNS

ALTERNATIVE EGGS PATTERNS

flowered stool

Resembling tile, this mosaic design is created with patterned paper, allowing you to easily match your decor. See more abstract designs on pages 162–165.

supplies

Unpainted crafts stool with an
  11-inch-diameter top
Sandpaper; tack cloth
White gesso; paintbrush
Crackle medium
Acrylic paints in periwinkle
  blue and light gray-green
Tracing paper; pencil; scissors
Tape; silver quilter's pencil
12-inch square scrapbook
  papers in three floral patterns
Decoupage medium, such as
  Plaid Royal Coat
Acrylic spray varnish

what to do

1 Sand the stool smooth. Wipe away sanding dust with a tack cloth.

2 Apply a coat of gesso to the stool. Let dry. Follow crackle medium directions to crackle only the edges and legs of the stool, using periwinkle blue as a base and light gray-green as a topcoat. Let dry.

3 Trace the stool top to tracing paper. Trace patterns, *pages 162–165.* Carefully cut out flower centers (see Photo A, *above right*). Tape the patterns on the stool. Trace shapes with the silver pencil (see Photo B). Set patterns aside.

4 Cut out the floral shapes. Trace the outline to the stool top. Cut, trace, and transfer all patterns to the stool top.

5 Hold the cutouts on scrapbook paper and cut out shapes. Arrange designs on stool top, slightly trimming shapes for paint to show between paper pieces. Cut and fit together a few pieces at a time until all pieces are together.

6 Brush decoupage medium onto the stool

continued on page 162

161

top and onto the back side of the papers. Adhere papers to the stool a few at a time to cover the top. Let the decoupage medium dry.

7 Apply several coats of decoupage medium to the stool top (see Photo C, *right*), allowing each coat to dry before applying another coat.

8 In a well-ventilated work area, spray the stool with varnish to seal. Let the varnish dry.

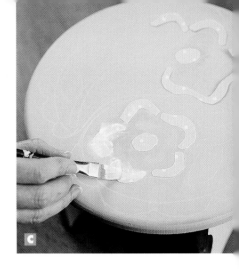

ALTERNATIVE STOOL PATTERN

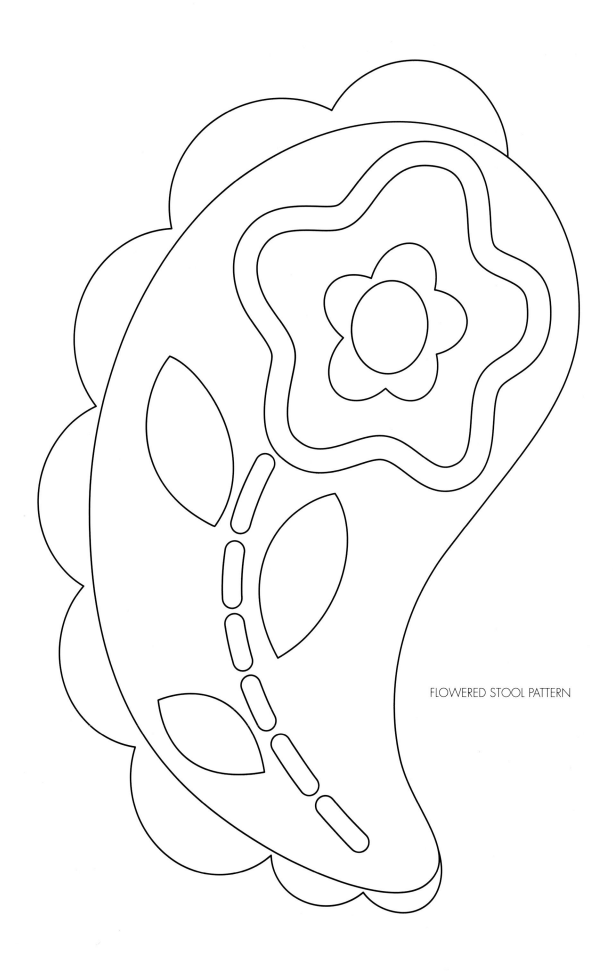

FLOWERED STOOL PATTERN

ALTERNATIVE STOOL PATTERN

ALTERNATIVE STOOL PATTERN

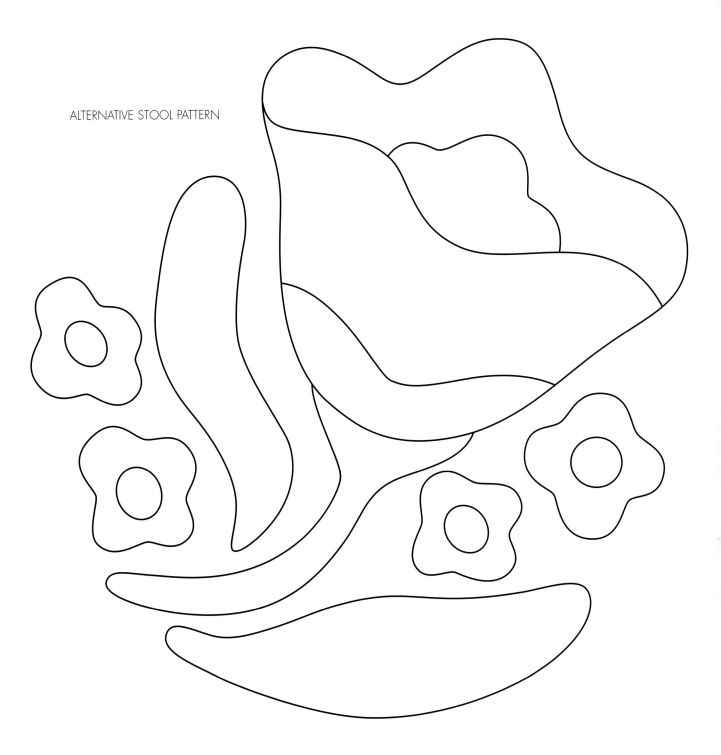

6 *more ways to use the stool patterns:*

- *Cut the shapes from felt to appliqué on a plain denim vest.*
- *Use embroidery stitches to outline a motif on a pillowcase.*
- *Appliqué fabric designs to a set of bath towels.*
- *Enlarge a flower or paisley design to appliqué to a sweatshirt.*
- *Place the designs randomly, enlarged and reduced, on a tabletop and paint them.*
- *Cut pieces from paper and decoupage on notebook covers.*

spring-motif etched glasses

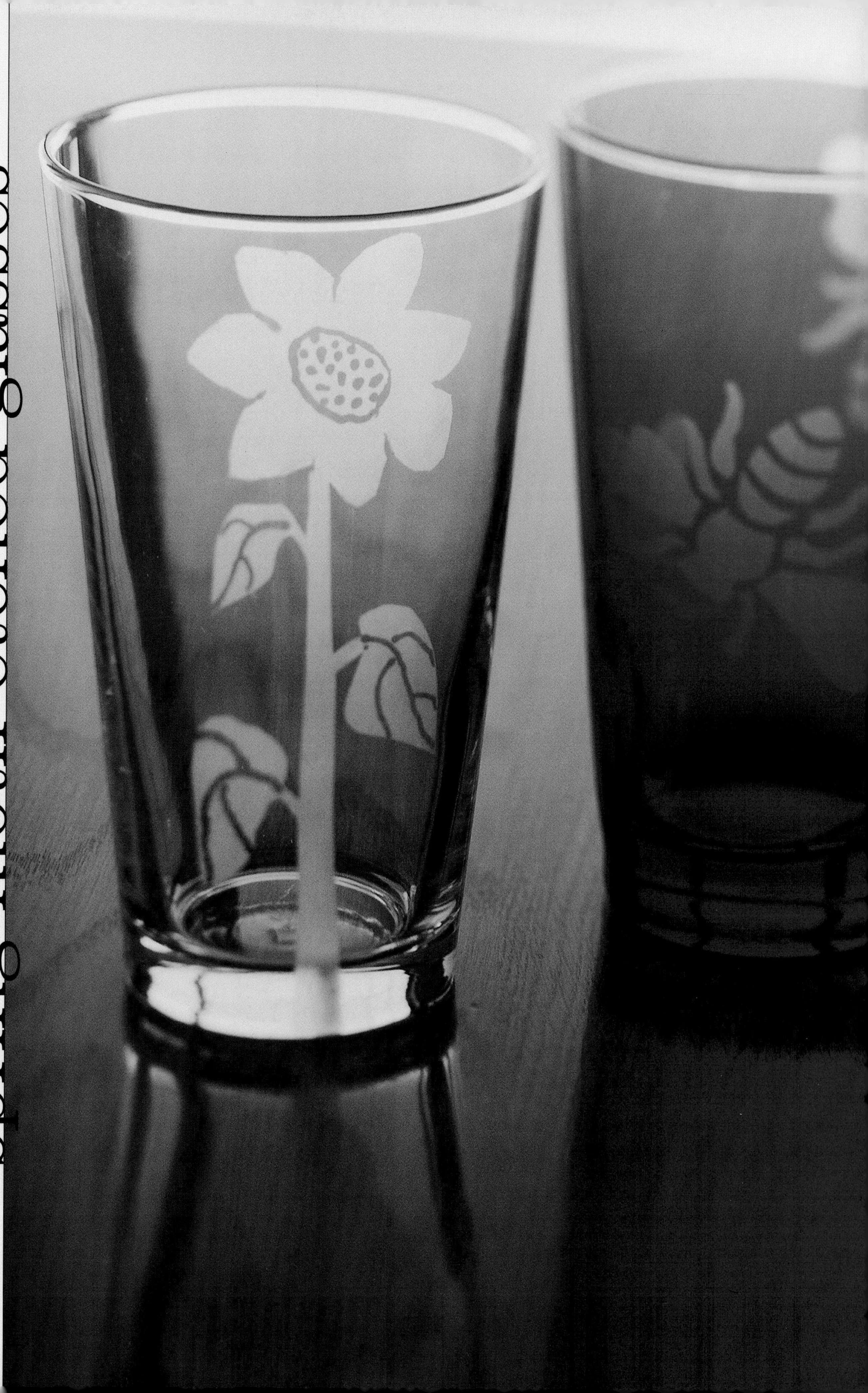

Easy-to-do etching showcases spring motifs on transparent tumblers. These and more patterns are on page 169.

supplies

Plain transparent glassware
White vinegar
Adhesive-back shelf paper
Carbon paper
Crafts knife
Spoon for burnishing
¼-inch adhesive vinyl letters
Fabric paint pen
Household gloves
Etching cream
Natural bristle paintbrush or
  sponge brush

what to do

1 Wash glasses with hot water and rinse with white vinegar. (Avoid touching the areas to be etched.) Cut a piece of adhesive-back shelf paper 1 inch larger all around than the chosen pattern, page 169.

continued on page 168

2 Use carbon paper to trace the pattern onto the shelf paper; cut out designs with a crafts knife (see Photo A, *right*). Set aside cutout portions. Peel backing from the negative or background portion. Place the negative portion on the glass, clipping edges as needed for the paper to adhere flat to the surface. Use the spoon to burnish (rub lightly) the design edges to prevent etching cream from seeping under the paper.

3 For the cat design, apply ¼-inch adhesive vinyl letters to spell "meow" in the word balloon. Use the paint pen to draw face details (see Photo B).

Allow the paint to dry several hours before etching. For the sunflower glass, use the paint pen to draw a center circle, dots for seeds in the circle, and petal divisions, using the pattern, *opposite*, as a guide.

4 Wear household gloves. Brush on the etching cream (see Photo C) following the manufacturer's instructions. Allow to set; thoroughly rinse the glass.

5 Peel off the adhesive paper, paint, and lettering (see Photo D). Thoroughly wash and dry the glassware before using.

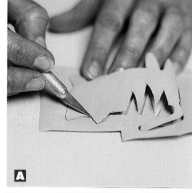

A

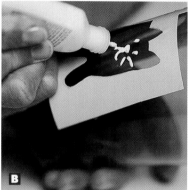

B

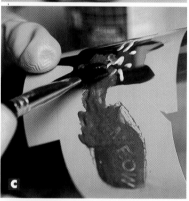

C

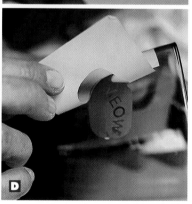

D

9 more ways to use the etched glasses patterns:

- *Make a stencil using the bee pattern; stencil it on a wall.*
- *Etch a vase using the sunflower.*
- *Paint a motif on a terra-cotta flowerpot.*
- *Etch the vine horizontally around the rims of glass tumblers.*
- *Cut the cat from felt and glue it to a child's photo album or diary.*
- *Cut shapes from paper and adhere to card stock to make greeting cards and gift tags.*
- *Enlarge the flower design, cut several blossoms, leaves, and stems from fabric, and appliqué a wall hanging.*
- *Etch a pattern on a clear glass soap dispenser for the kitchen or bathroom.*
- *Etch a bee on the corner of a wide glass picture frame.*

SPRING-MOTIF ETCHED
GLASSES PATTERNS

ALTERNATIVE ETCHED
GLASSES PATTERN

169

Plan a bouquet from the assortment of flowers and leaves, opposite. Adorn with beads and arrange on a brimmed hat for a spring-fresh topper.

supplies

Tracing paper; pencil
Scissors
Felt in assorted colors
Woven hat
Small beads
Thread; sewing needle
Embroidery floss

what to do

1 Trace and cut out floral and leaf patterns, *opposite*. Trace the shapes to felt and cut them out.

2 Using the photo, *above*, for inspiration, layer the felt pieces and arrange them on a hat. Maintain the arrangement and place the pieces on a work surface.

3 Thread a needle and knot the ends together. Sew the felt flower centers to the hat, using beads to secure each stitch. Attach the leaves using embroidery floss and running stitches.

170

EASTER BONNET PATTERNS

171

Trimmed with colorful wires and stickers that look like old-fashioned seed packets, these fun plant pokes brighten any windowsill. They take minutes to make, so whip up an entire collection from the patterns on pages 174–177.

supplies

Tracing paper and pencil
½- and ⅛-inch pine
Band saw
Medium-grit sandpaper
Wood glue
Drill and ⅛-inch drill bit
Acrylic paints in assorted colors
Paintbrush
18-gauge wire
Seed packets and stickers
Varnish, optional

what to do

1 Trace a pattern, *pages 174–177.* To make the plant pokes, transfer the large flowerpot pattern (with rim) to the ½-inch pine and the rim only to the ⅛-inch pine. Cut out the shapes; sand the edges.

2 Glue the ⅛-inch rim piece on the ½-inch flowerpot shape. Let the glue dry.

continued on page 174

3 Drill a hole in the bottom center of the plant poke. To trim the rim with wire, drill holes through the rim, using the patterns as guides.

4 Paint the wood shapes. Let the paint dry. Apply a second coat if needed and let it dry. Sand the edges of the painted wood for a worn appearance.

5 Using the photograph on *pages 172–173* for inspiration, lace wire through the drilled holes in the rim.

6 Apply a sticker to the front of the plant poke. Apply a coat of varnish if desired. Let the varnish dry.

7 Firmly push the wire into the bottom hole. Bend the wire into a spiral, zigzag, or other shape.

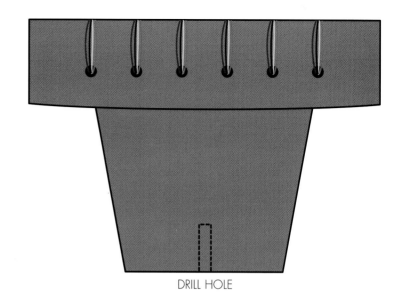

DRILL HOLE

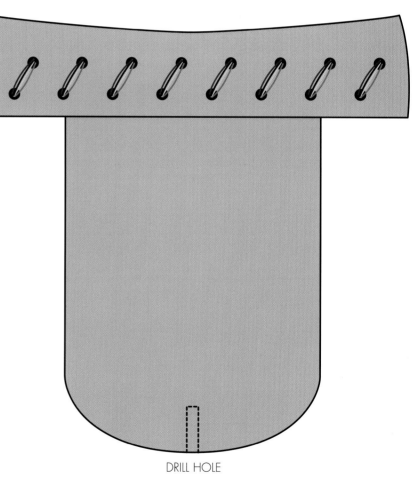

DRILL HOLE

DRILL HOLE

PLAYFUL PLANT
POKES PATTERNS

DRILL HOLE

DRILL HOLE

175

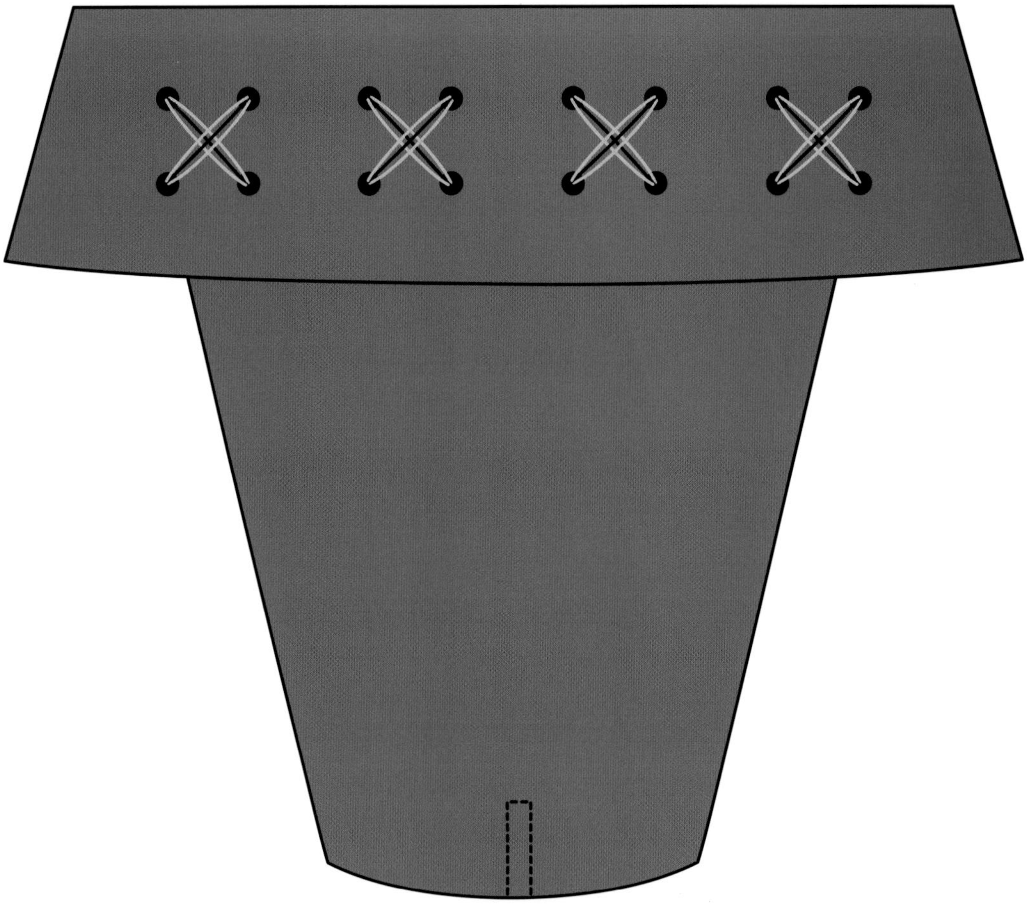

DRILL HOLE

PLAYFUL PLANT
POKES PATTERNS

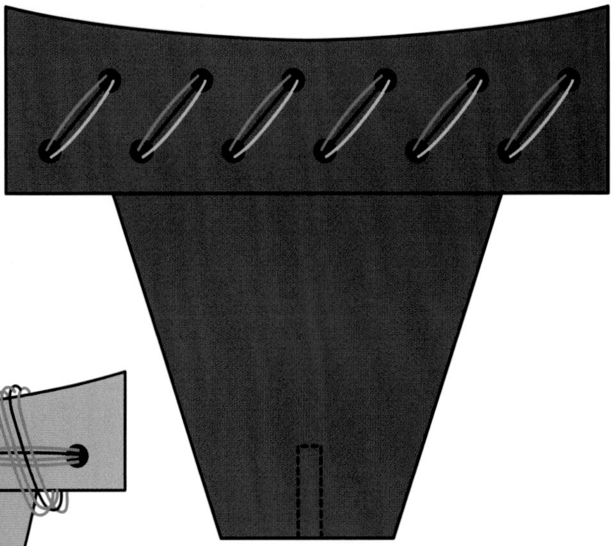

DRILL HOLE

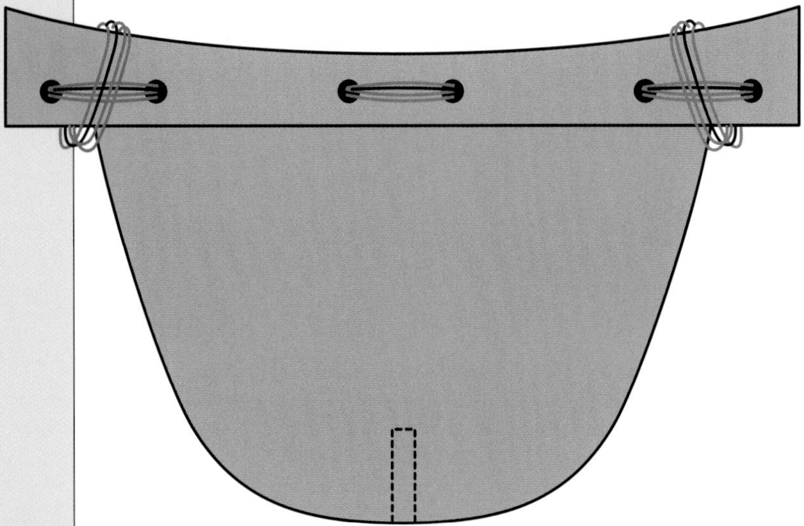

DRILL HOLE

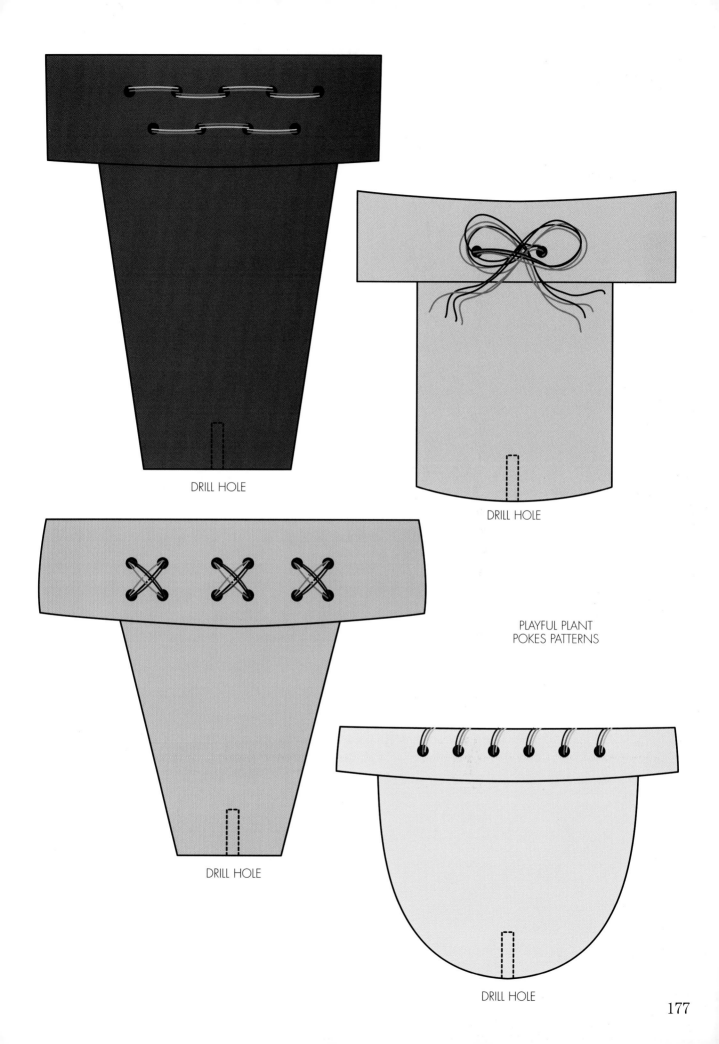

DRILL HOLE

DRILL HOLE

DRILL HOLE

PLAYFUL PLANT
POKES PATTERNS

DRILL HOLE

177

178

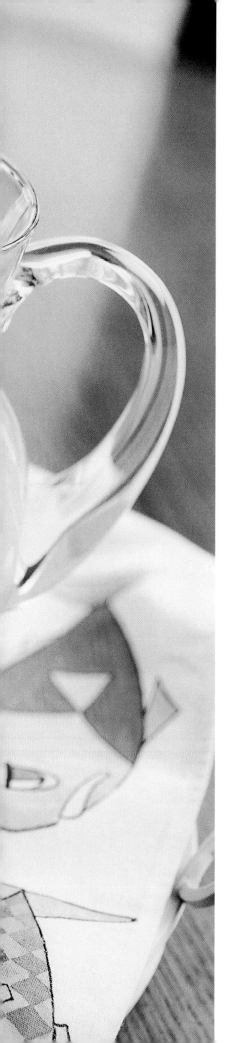

*What could be more
sensational than a
school of friendly
fish? Catch all your
favorites, pages
180–183, to create
a swimmingly cool
table set.*

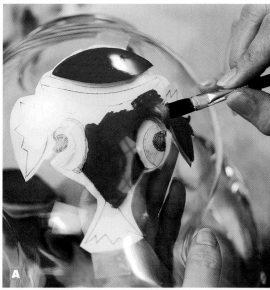

supplies

*Glass pitcher and glasses
Tracing paper; sharp lead pencil
Scissors; tape
Glass paints
Paintbrushes: medium round,
 flat, flat stiff bristled fabric
 brush, and fine liner
White cotton napkin
 (prewashed, dried,
 and pressed)
Light box for tracing, if desired
Fabric painting medium
Acrylic paints
Disposable plate
Black permanent paint pen*

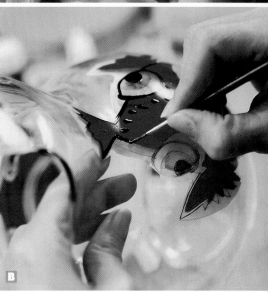

what to do

1 For the glassware, wash and dry the pitcher and glasses. Trace and cut out the patterns, *pages 180–183.* Avoiding the rim area, tape the tracings to the inside of the glassware.

2 Paint the sections using glass paints (see Photo A, *above right*). Let the paint dry.

3 Outline the fish with a fine liner brush and black glass paint (see Photo B). Let dry at least 24 hours before using.

continued on page 180

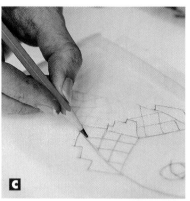

C

D

4 For the napkin, trace and cut out patterns, *pages 180–183.*

5 Tape the tracing on a light box or a sunlit window. Place the fabric over the traced design, tape it in place, and trace with a sharp lead pencil (see Photo C).

6 Mix one part fabric painting medium to two parts acrylic paint on a disposable plate. Pour in enough water to make a mixture the consistency of light cream. Using the drawn lines as guides, paint in the designs (see Photo D). Let the paint dry.

7 Outline the fish paintings with black paint pen. Let dry.

FISH PITCHER AND ACCESSORIES PATTERNS

FISH ACCESSORIES PATTERNS

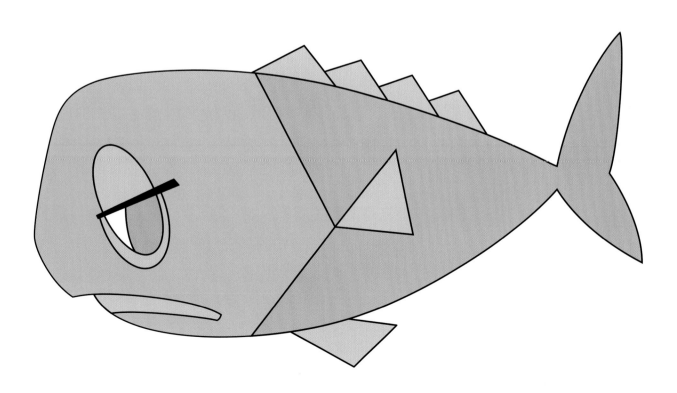

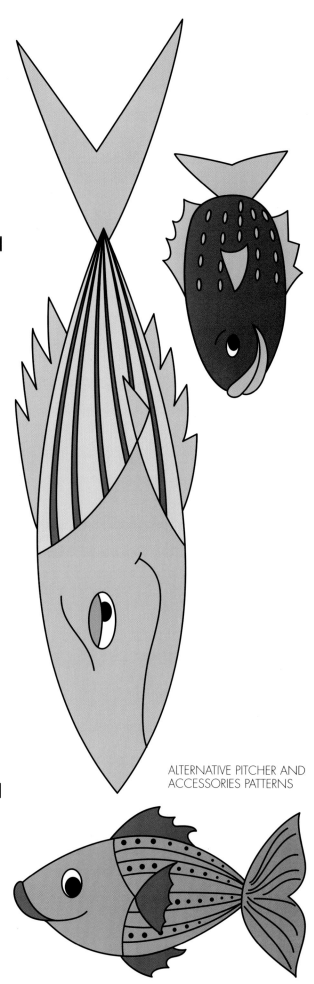

ALTERNATIVE PITCHER AND
ACCESSORIES PATTERNS

13 more ways to use the pitcher and accessories patterns:

- *Use fabric paint to enhance a pair of canvas sneakers with fish. Glue on rhinestone "bubbles."*
- *Paint the characters on a beach bag.*
- *Paint one fish on a sun visor.*
- *Use metal paints to make a school of fish on a metal sand pail.*
- *Transfer a border of fish to a wall and paint the designs with acrylic or wall paint.*
- *Cut large fish pattern pieces from fabric and appliqué on a canvas tote. Detail with embroidery stitches.*
- *Appliqué a fish on a hand towel.*
- *Use glass paints to paint fish on a ceramic toothbrush holder.*
- *Copy the fish patterns on black and white paper and make into a mini coloring book for your little ones.*
- *Enlarge a fish pattern onto card stock (at a copy shop). Color the fish and use it as a place mat.*
- *Transfer the fish patterns to your bathroom wall and paint with wall paints.*
- *Transfer the patterns to the outside of an aquarium. Paint with non-bakeable glass paints.*
- *Transfer three of the smaller fish to the front of a card. Using colored glitter, color in the solid areas of the fish with glue and glitter.*

FISH ACCESSORIES PATTERN

ALTERNATIVE PITCHER AND
ACCESSORIES PATTERNS

Plant a row of posies along the scalloped edge of a valance. Create the mottled background by spraying on stripes of paint; seed beads and cording finish the topper. Single out one of the florals, pages 186–189, for a spring-into-summer finish for your windows.

supplies

Paper; pencil; scissors
Unlined valance with straight bottom; measuring tape
1-inch-wide blue masking tape
Waxed paper; tracing paper
Acrylic paints in yellow-gold, bright pink, leaf green, mint green, pink, black, and assorted colors
Spray bottle

Tracing paper
Disposable plate
Liquid textile medium
Fine liner paintbrush
Large black seed beads
Black thread; needle
Lining fabric; straight pins
Thread to match lining
White satin cording

what to do

1 Cut a paper scallop pattern approximately 8 inches wide. Allowing ¼ inch of fabric along the lower edge of the valance, trace the scallop pattern.

2 Refer to the photo, *opposite,* and use masking tape to tape off 3-inch vertical stripes. Tape off the tab area if desired.

3 Cover a work surface with waxed paper. Lay the valance, right side up, on waxed paper. Mix yellow-gold paint with textile medium, following manufacturer's directions. Place about ½ cup of the mixture in a clean spray bottle. Spray the valance with the paint mixture to achieve a mottled effect (see Photo A). Let dry. Peel off the masking tape.

4 Trace and cut out a floral pattern, *pages 186–189.* Transfer the pattern to the valance, altering the position of the leaves for a random effect.

5 Lay the valance on clean waxed paper. On a disposable plate, mix small puddles of bright pink, leaf green, pink, and mint green paints (or color of your choice) in separate areas with textile medium; paint the flowers and leaves. Let the paint dry.

6 Mix black paint with textile medium. Use a fine liner paintbrush to detail the flowers and leaves. Let the paint dry. Sew three black seed beads in each flower center.

7 From lining fabric cut a piece ½ inch larger all around than the valance. Trim the valance ¼ inch beyond the scallop line. Trace the scallop pattern along a long edge of the lining and cut along the line. Right sides facing, sew together the scallop edges of the valance and lining. Clip the seam allowance, turn right side out, and press. Fold the sides of the lining to meet the valance side edges; press and pin in place. Hand-sew the edges together. Tack the upper edge of lining to the valance below the tabs.

8 Tack cording along the scallop edge of the valance.

A

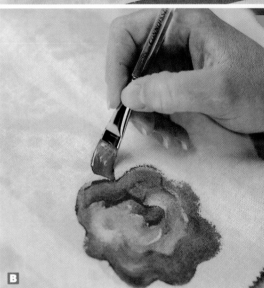
B

185

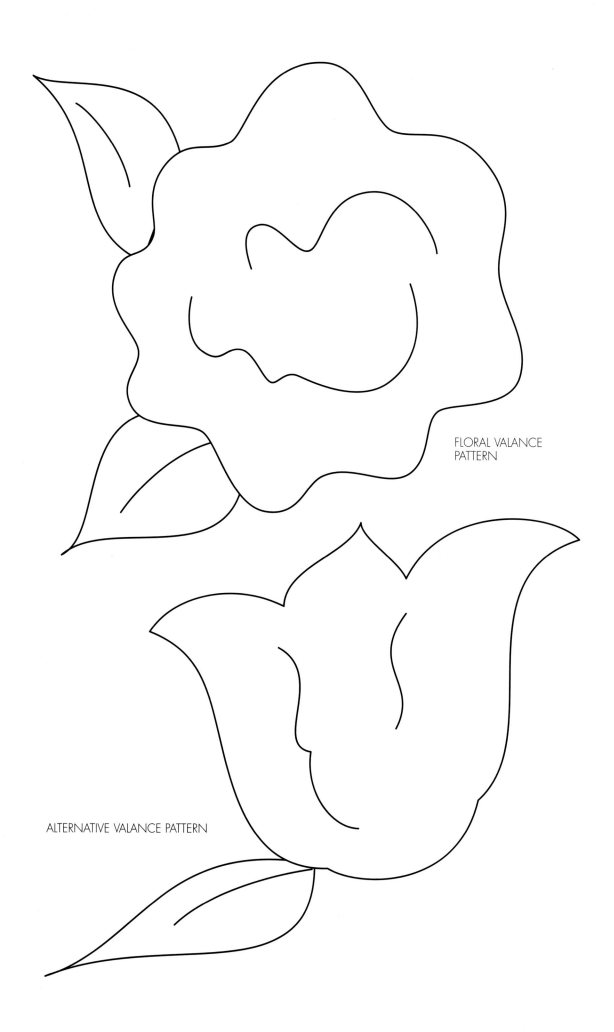

FLORAL VALANCE
PATTERN

ALTERNATIVE VALANCE PATTERN

ALTERNATIVE VALANCE PATTERNS

ALTERNATIVE VALANCE
PATTERNS

ALTERNATIVE VALANCE
PATTERNS

189

little ladybug tiles

You won't mind these silly bugs inching their way along the backsplash! Select from the bug, butterfly, and snail patterns on page 193 and paint them to coordinate with your kitchen or bath.

supplies

Small matte finish tiles
  (available at home stores)
Tracing paper; tape
Pencils with soft and hard leads
Glass or ceramic paints in
  blue, green, orange, pink,
  red, and yellow
Small round and flat
  paintbrushes
Fine black permanent marker
Medium-point black paint pen
Soft cloth
Spray- or brush-on glaze sealer
Tile glue; grout

what to do

1 Wash and dry the tiles according to the paint manufacturer's directions. Avoid touching the areas to be painted.

2 Trace patterns, *page 193*, to tracing paper. Using a soft lead pencil, color the back of the traced designs. Tape a pattern to a tile and trace the design with a sharp hard lead

continued on page 192

ladybug tiles patterns

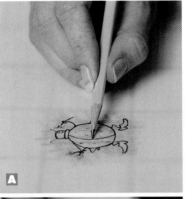

A

B

pencil to transfer drawing to the tile (see Photo A, *above*).

3 Remove the pattern. Paint the design with a small round brush, using the painting color guides, *below*. Let the paint dry.

4 To paint tiles solid colors, thin glass paint just enough to make it transparent. Use a flat brush that best fits the area to paint the tiles. Let the paint dry.

5 Outline and detail the designs with a black marker (see Photo B). Use a medium-point black paint pen to make dots. Let dry.

6 After the paint is dry, wipe off visible pencil marks with a soft, damp cloth. To seal individual tiles before applying them to a wall surface, spray several very light coats of glaze sealer on the tiles, allowing drying time for each coat. (Note: If sealer is sprayed too heavily, the glaze pools on the surface and causes some marker ink to dissolve and run.) For tiles mounted and grouted on wall surfaces, use brush-on glaze sealer rather than spray. Brush lightly and avoid excessive brushing back and forth. Let the sealer dry.

7 Glue tiles in place according to the tile manufacturer's directions. Allow glue to set. Because grout is abrasive and can scratch the painted tiles, avoid applying excessive grout on the tile faces while filling in the tile joints as well as possible. Let the grout dry. Carefully wipe the tile surfaces with a soft, damp cloth.

NOTE: *For regular cleaning, wipe tiles gently with a soft, damp cloth. Use nonabrasive cleansers.*

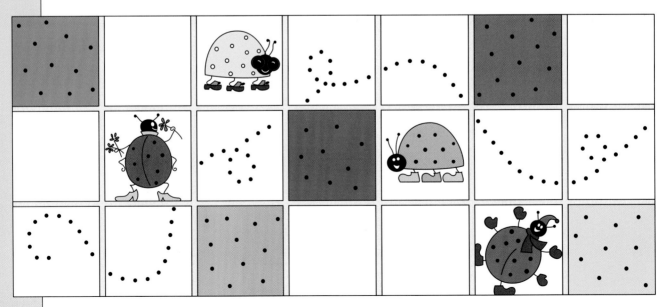

PAINTING COLOR GUIDES

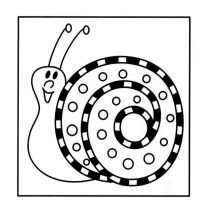

LITTLE LADYBUG TILES PATTERNS   ALTERNATIVE TILE PATTERNS   ALTERNATIVE TILE PATTERNS

pretty posy basin

As glorious as a field of wildflowers, this hand-painted sink bursts with nature's best colors. Fill a powder room basin with blooms and bugs using all, or a select few, of the patterns from page 197.

supplies

Ceramic sink
Tracing paper; soft lead pencil
Scissors; tape
Paintbrushes
Surface conditioner for
* painting glass*
Ceramic paints in white, blue,
* purple, light green, medium*
* green, dark green, pink,*
* and black*
Clear gloss glaze

tips before you begin

Choose a ceramic basin sink in nearly any color, size, or shape; adjust the pattern designs, *page 197*, to fit. Although a biscuit-color basin provides a neutral background for the paint colors shown, white or dark color backgrounds work just as well with altered paint colors.

Place an uninstalled basin on a work surface. Place old rolled towels around the basin to prevent it from rolling or shifting while you paint. Or cut a hole in a heavy cardboard box (such as the basin's shipping box) to create a temporary countertop; set the basin in the box while painting. If the faucet is installed,

continued on page 196

pretty posy basin patterns

securely tape a plastic bag over it; tape the drain mechanism to avoid dripping paint on it.

Use the patterns in the sizes shown, *opposite*, reduce or enlarge them, or use the patterns as inspiration to draw freehand florals and insects. While painting, quickly rework a painted area if needed by wiping off the wet paint with a damp cloth.

what to do

1 Wash and dry the basin according to the paint manufacturer's instructions. Avoid touching the areas to be painted.

2 Trace and cut out the patterns, *opposite*, from tracing paper. Tape patterns to the basin to determine design placement based on basin size and shape. Remove the pattern pieces. To transfer the designs to the surface, use a soft lead pencil to darken the paper on the back side of the designs. Tape the patterns, design facing upward, in the basin. Use a pencil to trace over the design lines, transferring the designs to the basin (see Photo A, *right*). Check the designs to determine whether all lines have transferred; remove the patterns from the basin.

3 Generously apply surface conditioner with a clean, dry paintbrush to

the outlined areas, (see Photo B). Let the conditioner dry. Paint designs within four hours of applying the conditioner, or reapply the conditioner before painting.

4 Begin painting the dragonflies, referring to the photo, *page 195*. Paint the wings and body white (see Photo C). While the paint is wet, blend in blue and purple shadows (see Photo D). Paint leaves and flowers in the same manner. Paint a vine using two or three shades of green. Paint small round purple and pink flowers by dipping a round paintbrush into both colors and applying the brush with a dotting motion onto the basin. Let the paint dry.

5 Apply narrow black shading lines and design details to the flowers and insects (see Photo E). Let the paint dry.

6 Apply one or more coats of glaze to the painted areas, allowing drying time for each coat. Allow the paint to air-dry for at least 10 days before using the basin.

NOTE: *Clean the basin only with nonabrasive cleansers. Avoid leaving water to stand in the basin.*

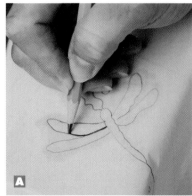

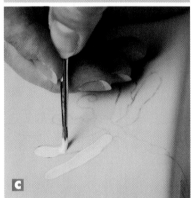

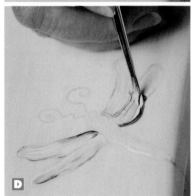

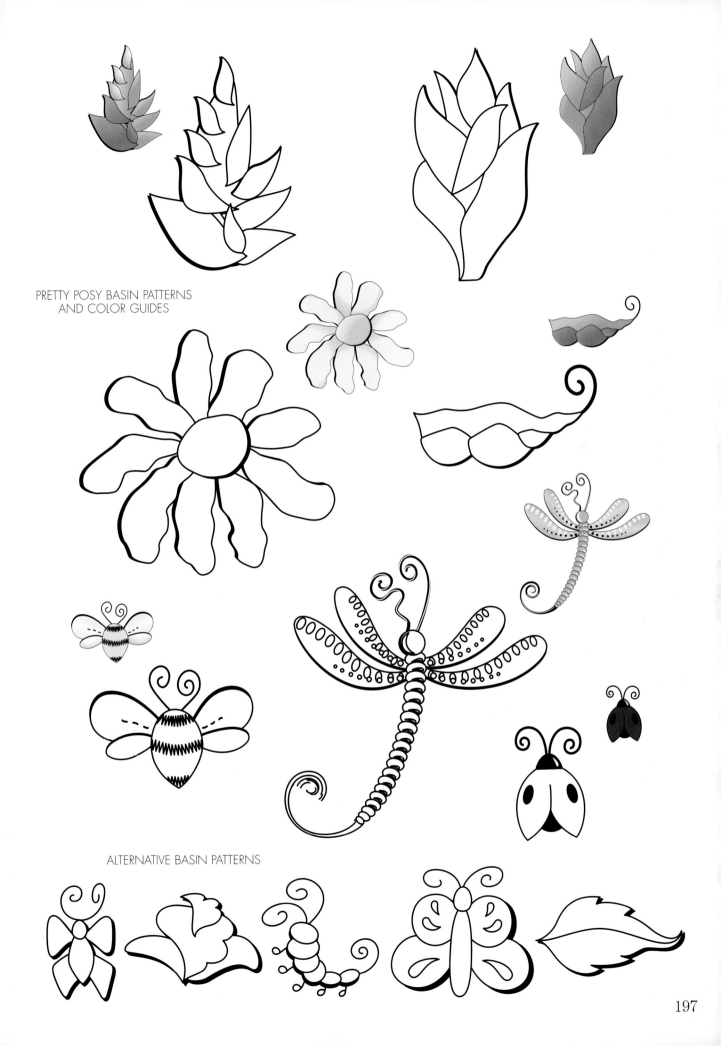

PRETTY POSY BASIN PATTERNS
AND COLOR GUIDES

ALTERNATIVE BASIN PATTERNS

*Dot the garden with colorful bricks for
unexpected surprises. Place these beauties
end to end for an edging or side by side for
stepping-stones. Select your favorite design
from the patterns on pages 200–201.*

supplies

Decorative brick
Newspapers
White spray primer
Acrylic paints for outdoor use
  in white, red, green, purple,
  yellow, and orange
Paintbrushes: medium round
  and fine liner
Tracing paper
Pencil with soft lead; tape
Fine-point black paint pen

what to do

1 Wipe the brick clean;
make sure it is dry. In a
well-ventilated work area,
cover the work surface with
newspapers. Spray the
brick with white primer. Let
the primer dry.

2 To make the design,
above, paint the top of
the brick white. Let dry.
Paint the sides red. Let dry.

3 Trace a pattern, *pages 200–201*, to tracing paper. Shade the back of the tracing with a soft lead pencil. Design side up, tape the tracing to the brick. Trace the lines with a sharp pencil to transfer the design to the brick (see Photo A, *right*). If the surface is too rough to transfer the lines, cut out and trace the patterns.

4 Using the painting guide on *page 200*, paint in all the designs. Use the fine liner brush to paint green vines. Paint purple stripes on the red sides of the brick. Let the paint dry.

5 Use a black paint pen to outline the designs (see Photo B). Draw a zigzag edge along the yellow border.

6 On the large flower, dot black on the tips of the flower petals by dipping the end of a large paintbrush handle in paint and applying it to the petal. Let the paint dry. Use a smaller paintbrush handle to apply yellow dots in the center of the black dots. Let the paint dry.

BRICK BEAUTY PATTERN

BRICK BEAUTY
PAINTING GUIDE

Yet
not one
of them is
forgotten
by God

paisley ladder

Dress up a stepladder with pretty paisleys in favorite colors. The artsy designs are on pages 204–205.

supplies

Small wood ladder
White spray primer
Soft lead pencil
Tracing paper; scissors
Acrylic paints in desired colors
Paintbrushes; white paint pen

what to do

1 Begin with a clean, dry ladder with any labels and stickers removed. In a well-ventilated work area, spray the entire ladder with primer. Let the primer dry.

2 Paint ladder steps and rails in coordinating colors. Let the paint dry.

3 Trace the paisley patterns, *pages 204–205*, to tracing paper. Cut out the shapes 1 inch beyond each design edge. Shade the back of the patterns with a soft lead pencil to transfer the designs to the ladder surfaces. For designs with intricate edges, cut away the edge from the pattern, draw a smooth line for the basic outline, and then freehand draw the fancy zigzag edge.

4 Place the patterns design side up on the ladder. Retrace the lines with a hard lead pencil to transfer the design (see Photo A). Remove the patterns.

5 Base-coat the shapes.

6 Paint contrasting color designs in each shape. Outline shapes with an opaque white paint pen (see Photo B). Let the paint dry. Draw dots, circles, stripes, and squares to finish the designs. Let dry.

PAISLEY LADDER PATTERNS

PAISLEY LADDER PATTERNS

try these ideas

15 more ways to use the ladder patterns:

- *Use the patterns to cut paper mosaics and decoupage a chair seat.*
- *Use fabric paint to transfer a design to the pocket of a denim shirt.*
- *Paint paisley motifs on the outside surfaces of a birdbath.*
- *Paint the designs on a wood porch floor.*
- *Use fabric paint to distinguish a throw rug with paisleys.*
- *Cut the patterns from paper; glue them to wood cutouts to make holiday ornaments.*
- *Photocopy mirror images of a design; paint each on wood for bookends.*
- *Paint the door of a wood cabinet with paisleys.*
- *Use fabric and appliqué the main patterns to a background; embellish with stitches and beads to make into a pillow.*
- *Paint designs in one corner of fabric dinner napkins.*
- *Paint the designs on a television cabinet or dresser drawers.*
- *Decoupage paper shapes to the lid of a photo box organizer.*
- *Cut the designs from paper and use as scrapbook embellishments.*
- *Paint the motifs on glassware using glass paints.*
- *Spruce up a basin by painting the details using permanent ceramic paints.*

beach treasure totes

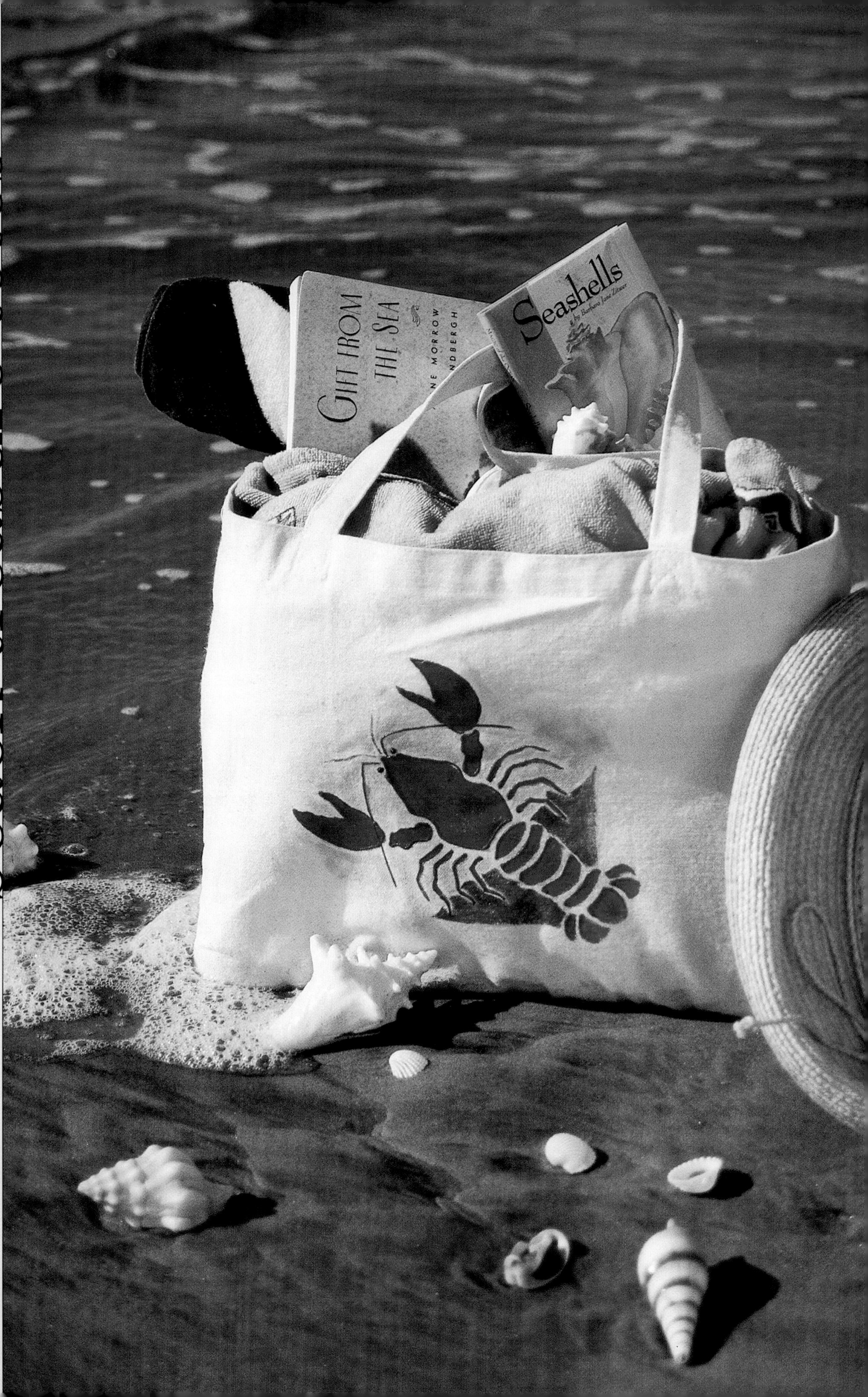

supplies

Tracing paper; pencil
Card stock or heavy paper
Cutting board; crafts knife
Cardboard
Canvas tote bags
Fabric paints in white, purple,
* blue, and other colors*
Small paintbrush
Tube-style dimensional paint in
* white or red*

what to do

1 Trace a pattern from
pages 208–211.
Transfer the pattern to card
stock or heavy paper. Place
the pattern on a cutting
board; use a crafts knife to
cut away the solid shapes,
creating a stencil.

2 Place cardboard in the
bag for a flat paint
surface and to prevent paint
from bleeding through to the
opposite layer. Center the
stencil on the bag; draw
around openings with a
sharp pencil.

3 Brush paint onto the
design areas. Use
white, purple, and blue to
paint a sunset around the
lighthouse or rippling water
surrounding the lobster.

4 Use tube-style paint in
white to outline the
lighthouse or in red to
outline the lobster. Let the
paint dry.

Stencil a hefty beach bag to tote towels,
lotions, and sandals to the beach—and
collect souvenirs. Utilize the patterns on
pages 208–211 to personalize several bags.

BEACH TREASURE TOTES PATTERN

BEACH TREASURE TOTES PATTERN

ALTERNATIVE TOTE PATTERNS

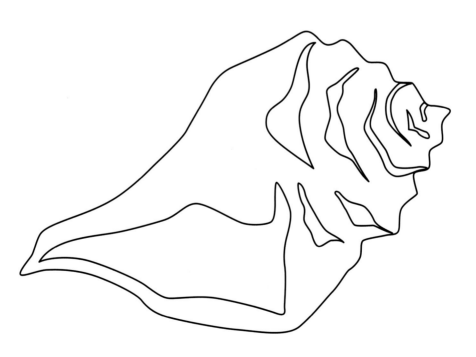

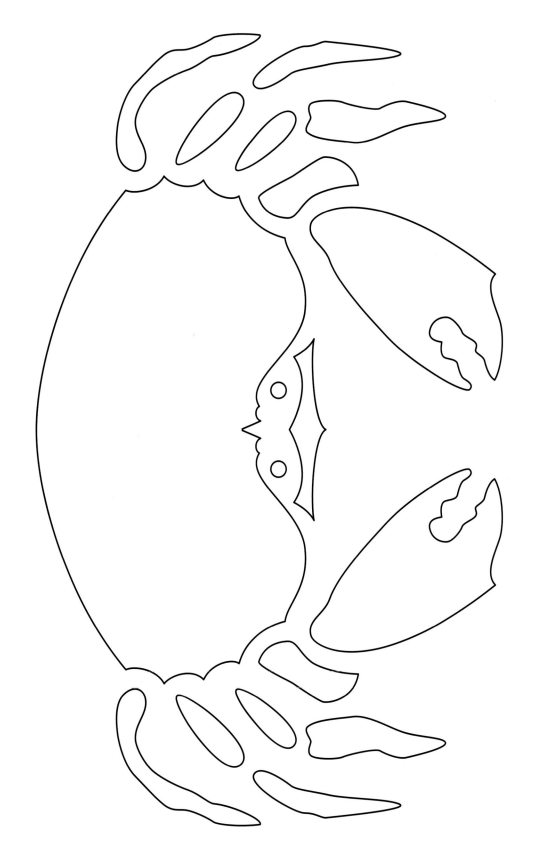

ALTERNATIVE TOTE PATTERN

Shining sequined fruit shapes give gift bags of all sizes summer zest. See more patterns on pages 214–215.

supplies

Tracing paper; pencil; scissors
Woven or paper bag
Thick white crafts glue
Sequins on strings

what to do

1 Trace and cut out a pattern, *below* or *pages 214–215*. Trace the pattern shapes to a bag.

2 Evenly and generously fill in the traced shapes with glue (see Photo A *right*), working on one area at a time.

3 Wind and press sequins in glue to fill the design with sequins (see Photo B). Let the glue dry.

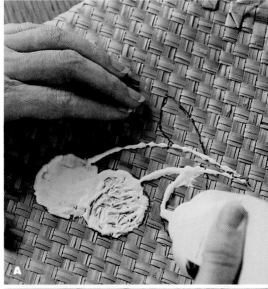

TREASURED GIFT BAGS
PATTERN

213

TREASURED GIFT
BAGS PATTERN

ALTERNATIVE GIFT
BAG PATTERN

ALTERNATIVE GIFT
BAG PATTERN

ALTERNATIVE GIFT
BAG PATTERN

215

Display your artistic talents on a kitchen trivet. Although these tiles are created with glass and ceramic paints, they have a watercolor appearance. Select from the fruit patterns, pages 219–221.

supplies

Tracing paper; black soft and
  hard lead pencils; tape
Ceramic tile
Paintbrushes: medium round
  and fine liner
Glass or ceramic paints in
  white, purple, dark green,
  magenta, olive green, red,
  and yellow ocher
Disposable foam plate
Water; toothbrush
Paper towels
Stand or easel for tile

tips before you begin

Many sizes and colors of floor tiles are sold at home improvement and flooring stores. If you plan to paint several tiles as gifts or for a backsplash, it is more economical to purchase tiles by the box.

For this project, a neutral tone tile was used; dark background tiles work as well and often eliminate the need for background painting.

The tile shown has a smooth surface; tiles that have more textured surfaces and an old-world look are often more difficult to paint.

For a vintage look on painted tiles that have dried thoroughly, lightly sand the surface with fine-grit sandpaper, revealing bits of the background.

To hang painted tiles, attach adhesive hangers on the back, use a plate hanger, or have the tile professionally framed.

what to do

1 Trace a pattern from pages 219–221. Shade the back side of the tracing with a black soft lead pencil. Tape the design, face up, on the tile. Trace the design with a

continued on page 218

hard lead pencil to transfer the design to the tile. If the tile surface is too rough to take the transfer, cut out the images and trace around them. Thin the white paint with water and fill in the design areas with a round brush (see Photo A).

2 Place pea-size dabs of paint on a plate. Thin the paint with water to the consistency of thin syrup. The paint should be a consistency slightly thicker than watercolors and should flow on nearly transparent.

3 Use a paintbrush to lay water on the background. Dip the brush in a paint color and blot the brush onto the wet background, allowing some tile background to show through the paint, as in Photo B. Apply paint loosely and sparingly at first with few brushstrokes, increasing the intensity for the desired effect. Allow adjacent paint colors to spread and blend. Let the paint dry.

4 To splatter the background, dip toothbrush bristles into a paint color, hold the brush parallel to the tile, and pull a finger across the bristles. Let the paint dry.

5 To paint fruit shadows, thin purple with water and add a tiny touch of dark green.

6 To paint the grapes, paint a base color of magenta, painting one grape at a time. While the paint is wet but beginning to soak in, apply purple shading (see Photo C). Consistently shade the top left of each grape. To prevent paints from running together, allow the paint to dry before painting an adjacent grape.

7 Base-coat the pineapple top dark green. Shade dark areas with purple (see Photo D). To create highlights on the pineapple top, clean the brush, dry it on paper towels, and brush off some of the green paint. Brush once, rinse the brush, and repeat for the desired effect. Randomly apply small spots of yellow ocher in the highlighted areas.

8 To paint the pineapple, use a full paintbrush and apply a smooth, even coat of yellow ocher over the pineapple oval. Apply paint generously to sit on top without immediately soaking in. While the paint is wet but has begun to soak in, apply shading by cleaning the brush, drying it on a paper towel, and dipping the brush into dark green. Lightly brush green on the left side to shade and shape. Use purple paint to shade and increase definition. While the ocher

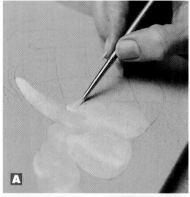
A

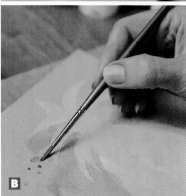
B

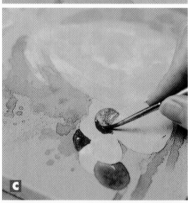
C

D

background is wet, paint the crosshatch lines dark purple. Let the paint dry.

9 Base-coat the apple red. While the paint is somewhat wet, shade with purple and a little dark green. Let the paint dry.

10 Use a fine liner with dark green and purple to apply shading and details to the fruit. Use white to apply nearly transparent highlights to the upper right portion of the pineapple, grapes, and apple as shown in the photograph on *page 216*. Let dry. Display on easel.

try these ideas

6 *more ways to use the tile patterns:*

- *Paint a design on prestretched canvas to hang on the wall.*
- *Paint a fruit and veggie border along a kitchen wall.*
- *Appliqué a wall hanging.*
- *Enlarge and paint a fruity design on corkboard to make a message center for the wall.*
- *Use fabric paint to color a design on a plain cotton kitchen towel.*
- *Paint your favorite fruit on a smooth knit cotton sweater.*

TROPICAL TILE PATTERN

ALTERNATIVE TILE PATTERN

11 *more ways to use the tile patterns:*

- *Paint a pattern on a clear glass pitcher using glass paints.*
- *Paint a design on a plain napkin holder.*
- *Use glass paint to create a design on a glass lampshade.*
- *Reduce the pattern, and appliqué fabric coasters.*
- *Use fabric paint to make designs on a kitchen apron.*
- *Cover a cookbook with paper, and glue paper fruit or veggie designs on the cover.*
- *Use fabric to appliqué a set of place mats.*
- *Appliqué designs to the corners of a fabric tablecloth.*
- *Appliqué designs to a fabric table runner.*
- *Reduce the patterns and draw on paper. Color with markers and use as gift tags when giving food gifts from the kitchen.*
- *Cut designs from wood for plaques; paint the shapes.*

ALTERNATIVE TILE PATTERNS

*Freshen up your kitchen with country
French flair for the table or windowsill
using these charming poultry patterns.
Plan your pail or planter using the
designs on pages 224–227.*

supplies

Tracing paper
Pencil
Scissors
Pressed cotton fabrics
Black adhesive-back
 crafts foam
Acrylic paints in red and yellow

Black tube-style fabric paint
Thick white crafts glue
Galvanized pail or oblong
 metal planter
Raffia

what to do

1 Trace and cut out patterns, *pages 224–227*, from tracing paper. Trace the paper patterns to fabrics. For patterns with multiple fabric pieces, cut out the shapes along the lines that meet an adjacent pattern shape.

2 Carefully smooth and press the fabrics on the crafts foam adhesive, aligning the pieces with multiple shapes. Cut out the fabric and foam shapes (see Photo A).

3 Use acrylic paint to paint the wattles and legs on the hen and rooster (see Photo B). Draw detail lines with fabric paint (see Photo C). Let the paints dry.

4 Glue the design to the pail or planter. Cut strands of raffia and glue them along the base of the planter to resemble straw.

COUNTRY ACCENTS PATTERNS

COUNTRY ACCENTS PATTERN

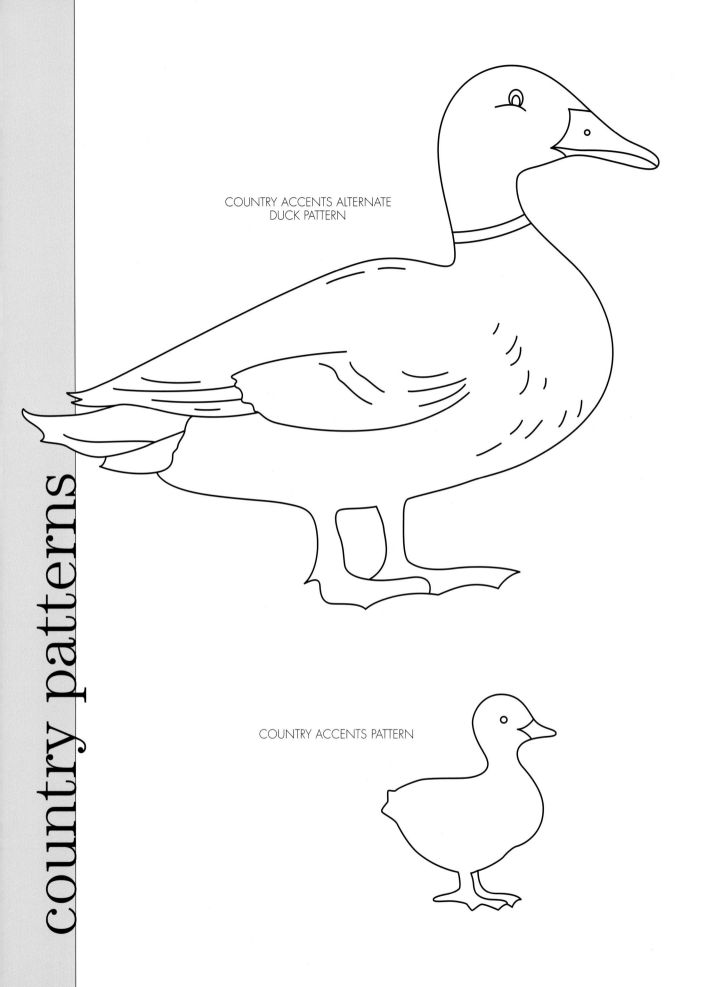

COUNTRY ACCENTS ALTERNATE
DUCK PATTERN

COUNTRY ACCENTS PATTERN

COUNTRY ACCENTS ALTERNATE
DUCK PATTERN

try these ideas

6 more ways to use the chicken accents patterns:

- *Transfer and paint the chicken shapes onto wood. Cut out, attach a dowel, and use as outdoor plant pokes in the garden.*
- *Transfer the patterns onto a purchased table runner. Paint with fabric paints. Group country items with your runner for a charming display.*
- *Reduce the patterns and transfer to the bottom of purchased muslin curtains or valance. Paint with fabric paints.*
- *Reduce the patterns if necessary and tape to the inside of a glass pitcher as a guide. Using glass paints, paint the outlines and let dry. Fill in the design with appropriate colors or with patterns for a more whimsical look.*
- *Trace the patterns on plain white paper for a child to color.*
- *Cut the chick pattern on page 224 from paper to make Easter cards.*

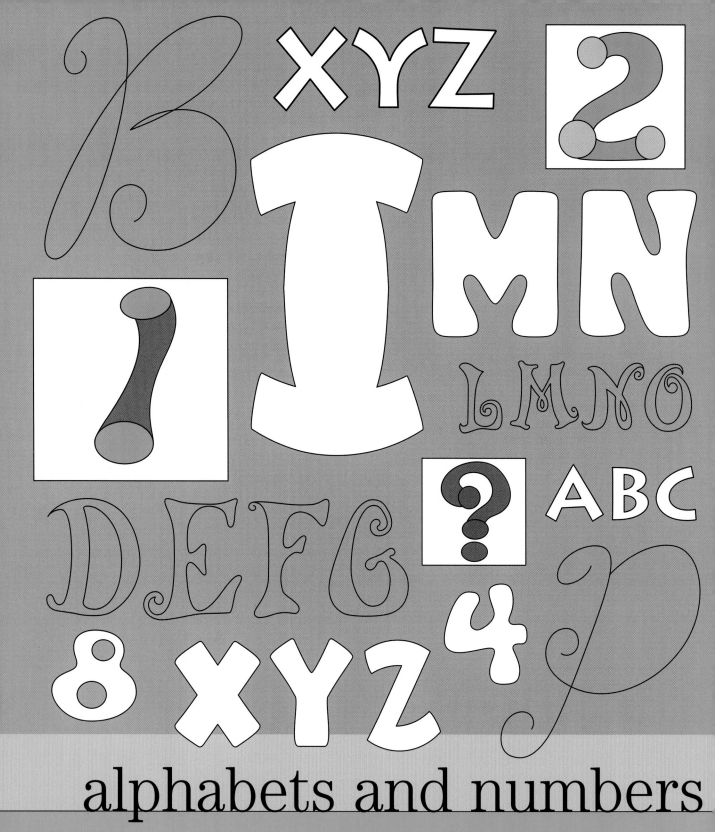

alphabets and numbers

One, two, sew a pillow for you! A, B, paint a mug for me! This pattern-packed chapter offers dozens of numbers and letters to get your creative juices flowing!

Keep these designs in mind anytime you want to personalize a craft for someone dear to your heart or for yourself!

equation pillows

Just right for a little mathematician's room, these pillows are a bright learning tool. More number, symbol, and punctuation patterns are on pages 232–235.

addition pillow
supplies
Assorted fabrics; scissors
Tracing paper; pencil
Fusible adhesive; iron
Sewing thread; pins
Muslin; poly-fil; batting
3 large buttons
Embroidery floss

Finished size 10×18 inches

what to do

1 Cut the fabrics:
1—6½×14½-inch yellow rectangle;
9—2½-inch blue squares for border;
10—2½-inch red squares for border;
2—2½×5-inch red strips for button border;
3—2½×5-inch blue strips for button border;
1—12×20-inch backing rectangle for quilting;
1—12×20-inch rectangle batting;
1—10½×21½-inch rectangle for pillow back.

2 Trace the numbers and symbols, *pages 232–235*, in reverse onto the paper side of fusible adhesive. Fuse to the wrong side of fabrics; cut out. Remove the paper backing and fuse to the yellow rectangle. Appliqué the shapes in place.

3 Refer to the photo, *opposite*, and sew together two red and one blue 2½-inch squares; press. Sew the unit to one narrow side of the rectangle; press. Sew two strips each with four red and four blue 2½-inch squares; press. Sew one to each long side of the rectangle; press. Sew together the two red and three blue 2½x5-inch strips, alternating color placement; press. Sew the unit to remaining raw edge of the yellow rectangle; press.

4 Layer the backing rectangle, batting, and pillow top. Quilt as desired.

5 Right sides together, layer the quilted pillow front and the rectangle for pillow back. Sew around three sides of the pillow cover, leaving the 5-inch button border section open. For a facing, turn under and stitch ¼ inch along the opening. Align the stitched edge with the pieced border seam; pin in place. On the front of the pillow cover, stitch-in-the-ditch to catch facing. Clip corners; turn pillow cover to right side.

6 To make the pillow form, cut two 12x16-inch rectangles from muslin. Sew the rectangles together with a ½-inch seam allowance, leaving an opening for stuffing. Turn to the right side, stuff with poly-fil, and sew the opening closed. Insert the pillow form into the pillow cover.

7 Sew on buttons to close the pillow opening, tying the floss on the top side of the buttons.

multiplication pillow
supplies

Assorted fabrics; scissors
Tracing paper; pencil
Fusible adhesive; thread; pins
2 yards cording; 8 buttons
Batting; poly-fil; muslin

Finished size 12x22 inches

what to do

1 From green fabric cut 1—4½x14½-inch rectangle; 2—2½x18½-inch strips; 2—2½x12½-inch strips. From assorted prints cut 2—2½x14½-inch strips; 2—2½x8½-inch strips; 2—2½x44-inch piping strips (diagonally piece the strips for one long strip); 2—15½x13-inch backing rectangles; 1—15½x13-inch batting rectangle.

2 Trace the numbers and symbols, *pages 232–235*, in reverse onto the paper side of fusible adhesive, eliminating the dots on the numbers. Fuse to the wrong side of fabrics; cut out. Remove paper backing; fuse to the green rectangle. Appliqué the shapes in place.

3 Sew the long print border strips to the green rectangle; press. Sew on the short print strips; press. Sew the green border strips to the print borders; press.

4 Layer a backing rectangle, batting, and pillow top. Stitch-in-the-ditch along the border seams.

5 To make the piping, fold the piping strip in half lengthwise around the cording, aligning raw edges. Stitch close to the cording. Align raw edges; pin and baste piping to pillow front.

6 To make an envelope opening for the pillow back, fold under and press ¼ inch and then 1½ inches along one narrow edge of each backing rectangle; topstitch close to the double folded edge. Right sides together, layer the backing rectangles on the pillow top, aligning raw edges and overlapping the hemmed edges at the

continued on page 232

pillow center. Pin in place. Sew the backing to the pillow top, catching piping seam in stitches. Clip the corners; turn the pillow to the right side.

7 Sew buttons on each numeral where indicated with dots on the pattern pieces.

8 To make the pillow form, cut two 14×24-inch rectangles from muslin. Sew the rectangles together with a ½-inch seam allowance, leaving an opening for stuffing. Turn to the right side, stuff with poly-fil, and sew the opening closed. Insert the pillow form into the pillow through the envelope closure.

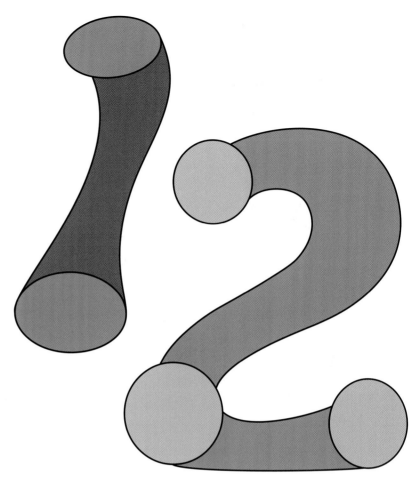

EQUATION PILLOWS
PATTERNS

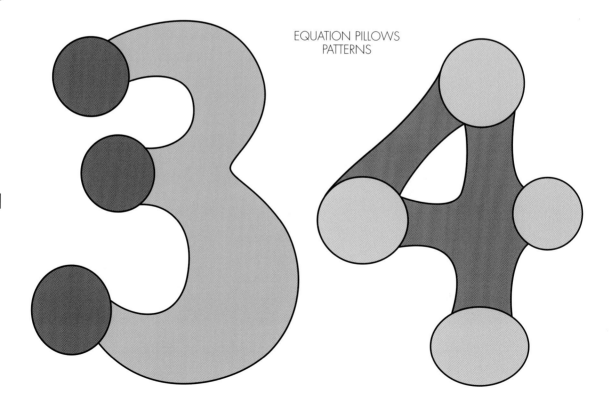

EQUATION PILLOWS PATTERNS

233

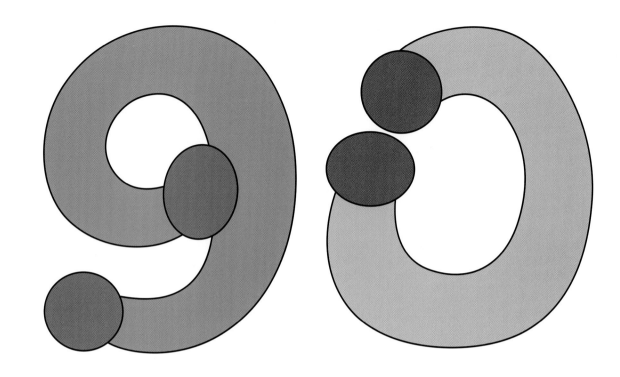

EQUATION PILLOWS PATTERNS

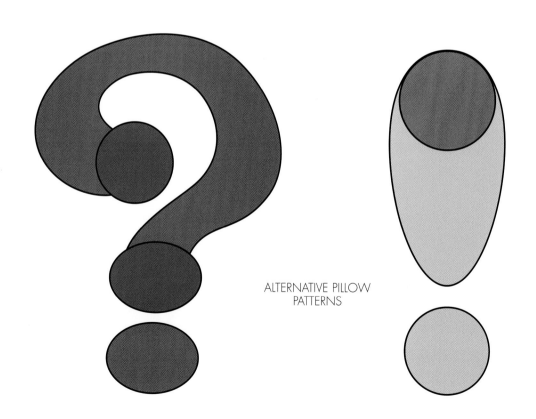

ALTERNATIVE PILLOW
PATTERNS

ALTERNATIVE PILLOW PATTERNS

13 *more ways to use the equation patterns:*

- *Appliqué a bed or wall quilt.*
- *Personalize the banding of a child's favorite blanket.*
- *Appliqué the front of a fabric-covered baby album or scrapbook.*
- *Appliqué a bib.*
- *Paint numerals on the backs of kid-size chairs.*
- *Paint a room sign on a piece of wood.*
- *Make a fabric book and appliqué the appropriate number of objects next to each number.*
- *Cut numbers, symbols, and punctuation from patterned scrapbook paper to make note cards.*
- *Appliqué a hand towel or beach towel.*
- *Label containers.*
- *Make stencils to use for decorating a birthday cake.*
- *Cut numbers from wood to make a house number sign.*
- *Use the patterns to paint numbers randomly on a child's playroom wall.*

Go team! Cheering from the stands or from an armchair becomes cozier with these fleece blankets. All the numbers and letters you need are on pages 237–247.

supplies

*2 yards each of 60-inch-wide
  fleece in two colors; scissors
Large round plate; pins
Yarn to match one fleece color
Tracing paper; pencil; scissors
Spray adhesive
Sewing machine; thread to
  match fleece*

what to do

1 Cut the salvages from the fleece. Use a large round plate to trace and cut rounded corners.

2 Pin the fleece layers together. Blanket-stitch (diagram, *page 69*) the edges with yarn.

3 Trace and cut out letters and numbers, *right* through *page 247*. Lightly spray the backs of the paper patterns with adhesive. Position the letters and numbers on the fleece.

4 Using a sewing machine with the feed dog lowered and foot pressure released, free-motion stitch around letters using a straight stitch or tight zigzag. Remove paper letters. Carefully cut through only the top layer of fleece just inside stitching line. Remove top layer to reveal the color beneath.

NAME BLANKETS
PATTERNS

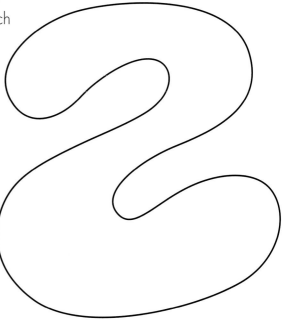

NAME BLANKETS
PATTERNS

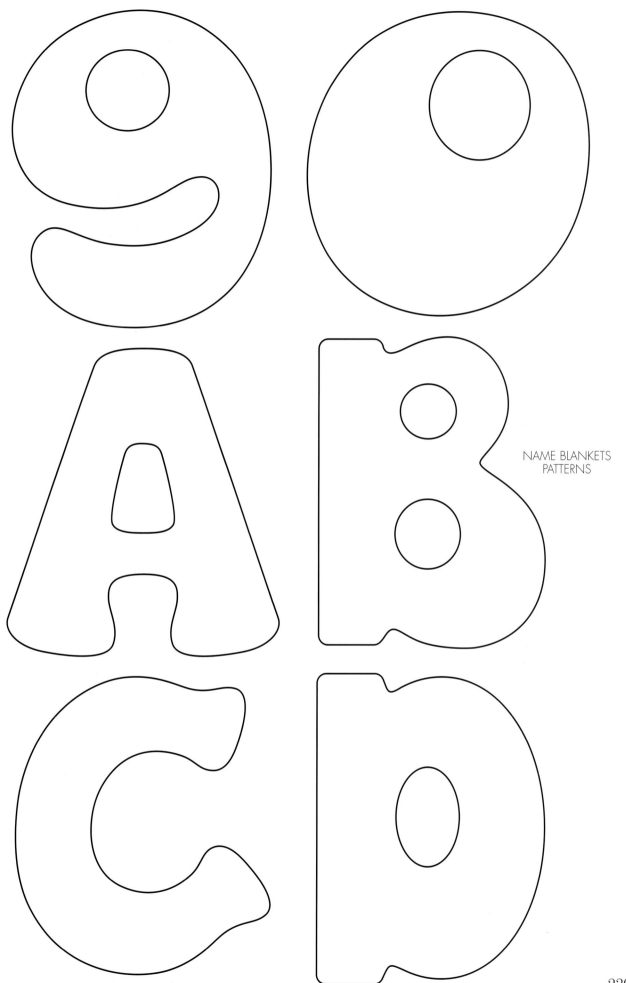

NAME BLANKETS
PATTERNS

NAME BLANKETS
PATTERNS

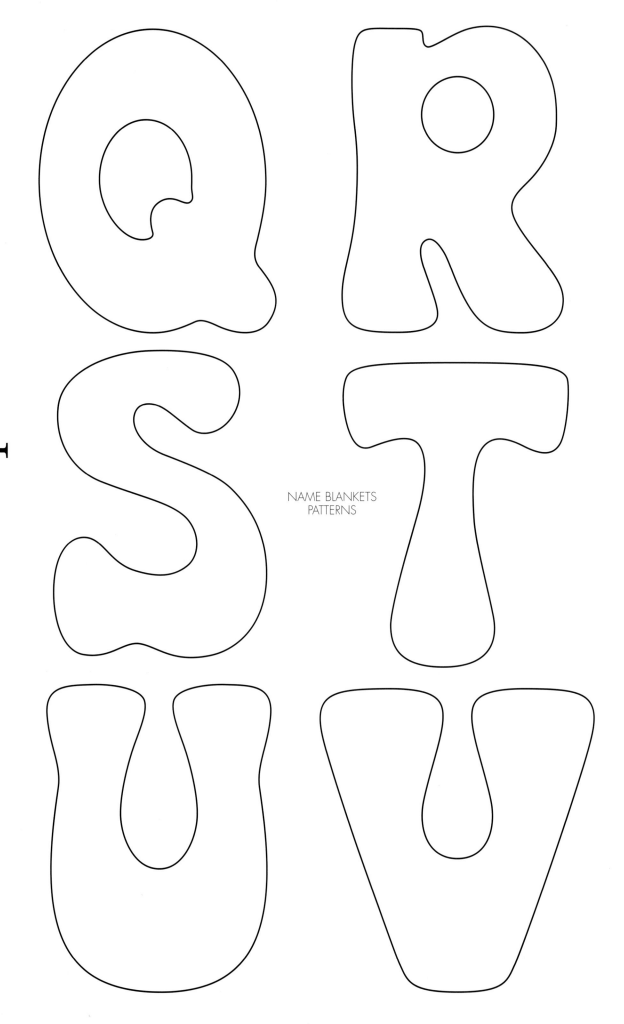

NAME BLANKETS
PATTERNS

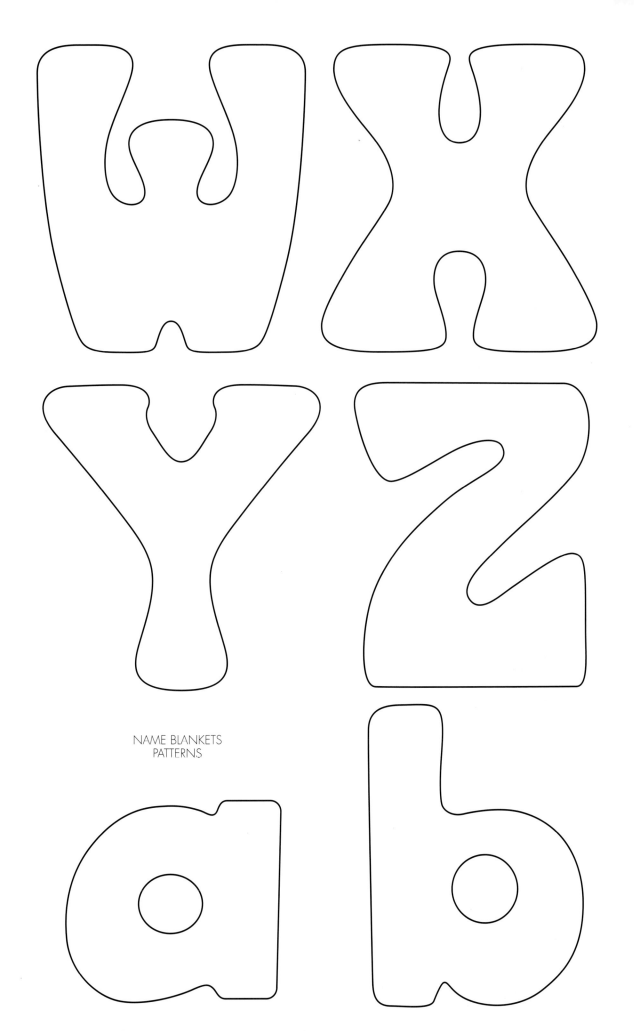

NAME BLANKETS
PATTERNS

name blankets patterns

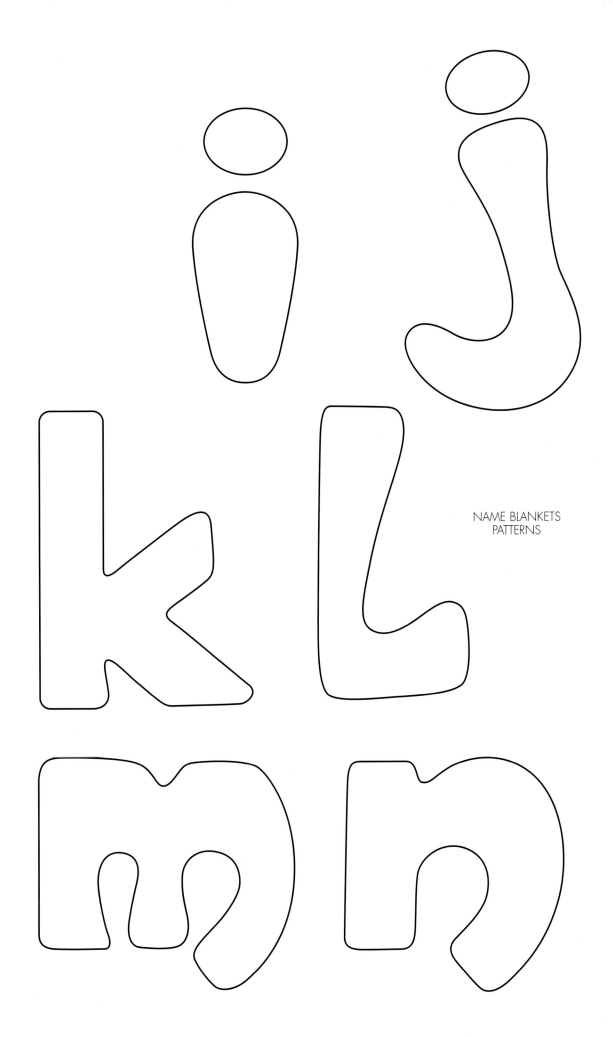

NAME BLANKETS
PATTERNS

NAME BLANKETS
PATTERNS

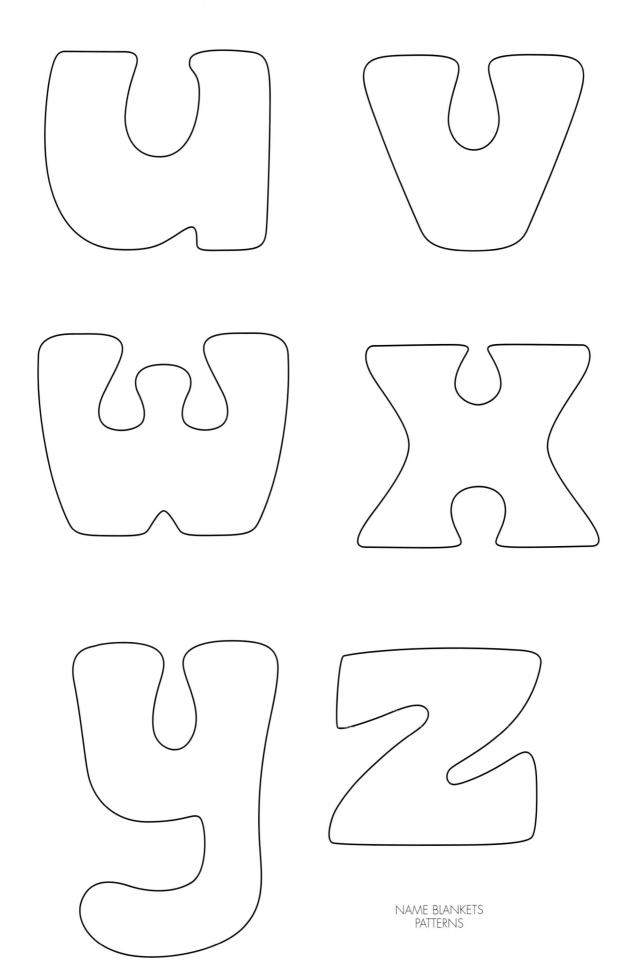

NAME BLANKETS
PATTERNS

*With two alphabets and over 20 mini motifs
to choose from, pages 249–253, painting
and personalizing a coffee mug is a snap.*

supplies

*Ceramic coffee mug with satin
  or matte finish
Tracing paper
Pencil; scissors
Acrylic enamel paints or
  glass paints
Paintbrushes: small flat, liner*

what to do

1 Wash and dry the mug.
Avoid touching the
areas to be painted.

2 Trace and cut out letters
and patterns, *pages
249–253*, from tracing
paper. Position and trace
the patterns below the rim
area of the mug.

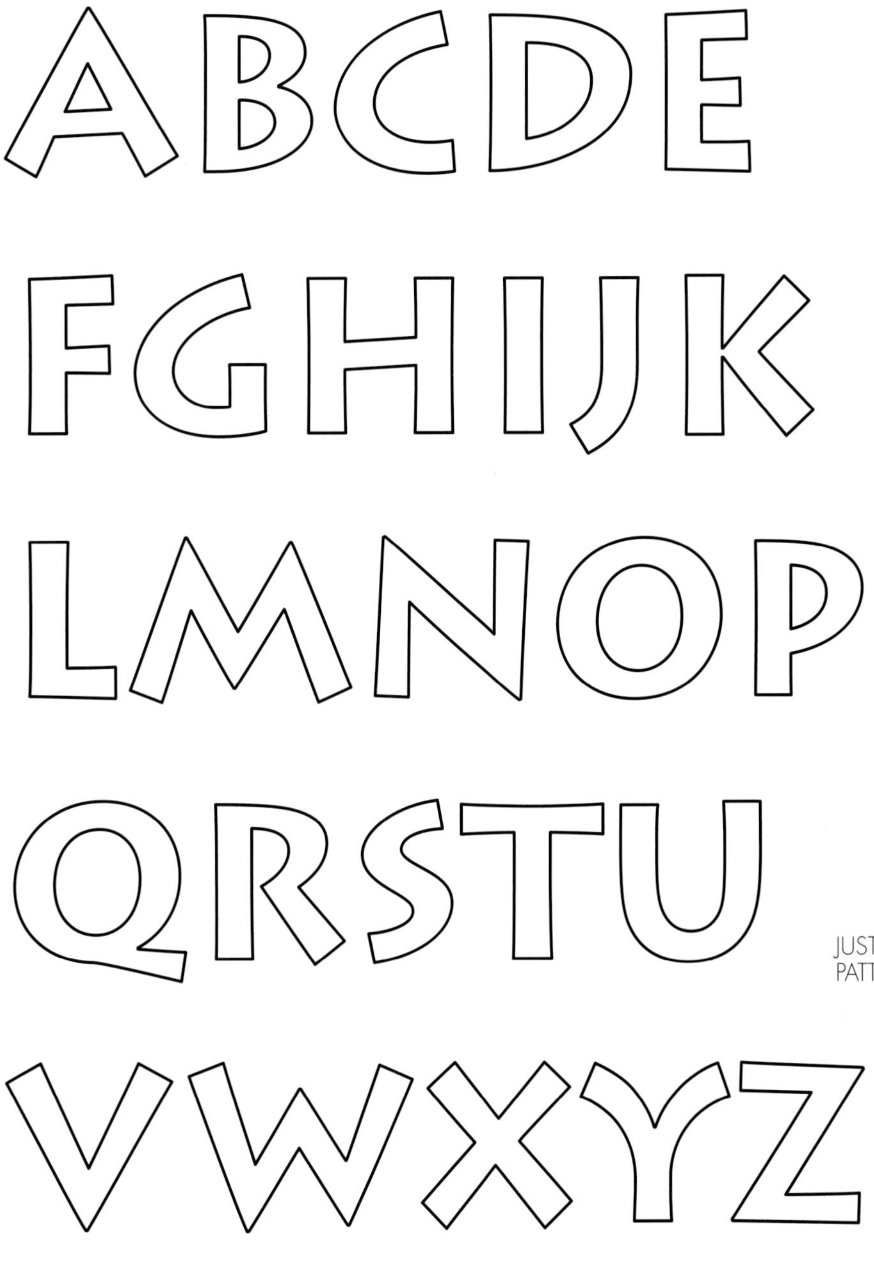
ABCDE
FGHIJK
LMNOP
QRSTU
VWXYZ

JUST-FOR-YOU MUGS PATTERNS

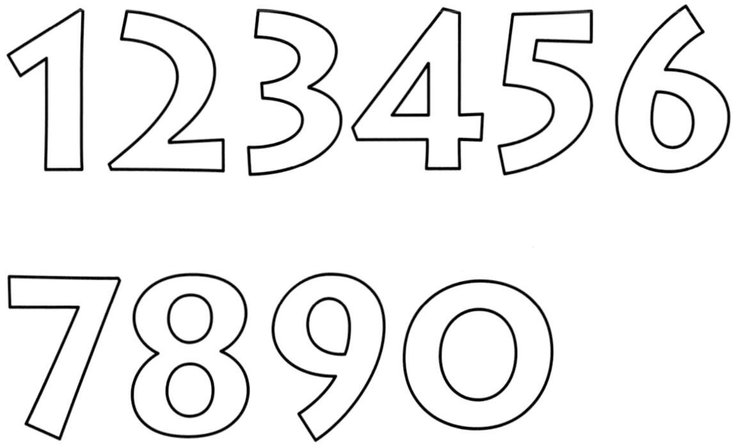
123456
7890

3 Paint letters with the small flat paintbrush, allowing drying time after each coat. Apply dots, stripes, or swirls with the liner brush. Let the paint dry for 24 hours.

4 Follow the paint manufacturer's directions to bake and cool the pieces.

JUST-FOR-YOU MUGS PATTERNS

JUST-FOR-YOU MUGS PATTERNS

JUST-FOR-YOU
MUGS PATTERNS

JUST-FOR-YOU
MUGS PATTERNS

joyous noel

Spell out holiday greetings on contemporary ornament shapes using the chunky alphabet, right and pages 256–257.

supplies

Tracing paper
Pencil
Scissors
Card stock in black, green, and red
Thick white crafts glue
Scrapbook eyelets and setting tool
Metallic silver marking pen
Ribbon
2 jingle bells
Needle; thread

what to do

1 Trace and cut out the ornament pattern, *right,* and the letters, *above right* and *pages 256–257.*

2 Use the patterns to cut four black hanger caps, four green ornaments, and one of each red letter.

3 Glue black caps on the ornaments. Use eyelets to attach the letters to the ornaments. Outline black caps with metallic silver.

4 Cut a piece of ribbon long enough to allow a hanging loop. Glue the ornaments on the ribbon.

5 Cut a length of ribbon and tie it in a bow at the lower end of the long ribbon. Sew jingle bells on the ribbon. Trim and turn up the lower end of the ribbon behind the bow. Tack in place. Fold over the ribbon along the top to make a hanging loop; tack in place.

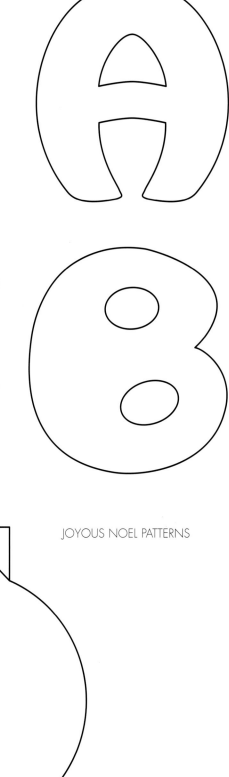

JOYOUS NOEL PATTERNS

JOYOUS NOEL
PATTERNS

JOYOUS NOEL
PATTERNS

Exquisite on a package or hung on the tree to reflect the lights, these beaded monograms are a personal and lasting insignia. Choose from the alphabet on pages 259–261.

supplies

Tracing paper; pencil
16 to 18 inches of
* 18-gauge wire*
Assorted beads
Needle-nose pliers
Artificial greenery or holly
Gold cording or ribbon
Scissors

what to do

1 Enlarge and trace an initial from the patterns, *below* and on *pages 260–261.* Using needle-nose pliers, roll a tight loop at the beginning of the wire to prevent beads from sliding off (see diagram, *right*). Bead the wire in a pattern of shapes, sizes, or colors. Roll a loop at the end of the wire to secure the beads. Bead short lengths of wire for letters with cross sections.

2 Use the traced pattern as a guide to shape the script letter. Wire cross sections to the larger letter shape. Attach large dangling beads to the end wires, if desired.

3 Adorn the letter with artificial greenery and tie on cording or ribbon for a hanger.

BEADED INITIALS ASSEMBLY DIAGRAM

BEADED INITIALS
ALPHABET

BEADED INITIALS
ALPHABET

BEADED INITIALS
ALPHABET

261

geometrics, stars, and

*The sky is the limit (and the inspiration)
for this star-studded chapter. Learn how to
top gifts with elegant stars, set a table with
signs of the zodiac, and give a lamp base*

the zodiac

pizzazz with simple circles. Whether you paint wood, cut paper, or sew fabric, the projects in this chapter will put a twinkle in your eye.

stand-up stars

Painted in colors of antique toys and lightly sanded for aged appeal, this collection of stars boasts trims of vintage buttons, homespun bows, and rustic wire.

supplies

Tracing paper; pencil; scissors
½- to 1-inch-thick pine
Band saw
Sandpaper; tack cloth
Newspapers
Acrylic paints in desired colors
Paintbrush; wood glue
Thick white crafts glue
Buttons; fabric scraps
Wire and wire cutters
Round pencil, small dowel,
  or wood skewer

what to do

1 Trace the star patterns, *opposite,* to tracing paper. To trace the half-star pattern, fold the tracing paper in half and align the fold with the dotted pattern edge. Cut out the shapes; open the folded paper. Transfer patterns to pine.

2 Use a band saw to cut on the pattern lines. Sand the wood edges smooth; remove sanding dust with a tack cloth.

3 Cover a work area with newspapers. Paint the stars on one side and the edges. Let the paint dry. Paint the opposite side of the star; let the paint dry. Apply additional coats of paint if needed; let the paint dry.

4 Lightly sand star edges for a worn, antique look. Wipe away sanding dust with a tack cloth.

5 For the stacked stars, layer a small star on a large one, using the photograph, *opposite,* as a guide. Use wood glue to attach the stars. Let the glue dry.

6 To adhere buttons, use thick white crafts glue and center a button on a star. Let the glue dry. For variety, layer and glue two or three buttons together or arrange and glue several small buttons on a star.

7 For a fabric bow, tear an approximately 1×12-inch strip from fabric scraps. Wrap the strip around the star and tie it in a bow. Apply glue to the fabric if desired; trim the bow ends.

8 For wire-wrapped stars, wrap a length of wire around a star between the star points; twist the wire ends together. Trim the wire to allow about 3 inches on each end. To coil the ends, wrap the wire around a round pencil, small dowel, or wood skewer. Remove the pencil or dowel.

STAND-UP STARS PATTERNS

*Turn ordinary lamps into dramatic
beacons using two coordinating paint
colors, a host of delightful designs, opposite,
and these easy painting techniques.*

supplies

*Lamp and shade
Plastic sandwich bags
Masking tape
Newspapers
White spray primer
Acrylic paints in desired colors
Disposable plate
Sea sponge
Paintbrushes
Pencil with round eraser*

what to do

1 Cover and wrap the lamp cord and hardware with plastic sandwich bags; tape the bags with masking tape.

2 In a well-ventilated room, cover the work surface with newspapers. Spray primer on the lamp base and the outside of the lampshade. Let the primer dry.

LIVELY LAMPS PATTERNS

3 To sponge-paint the base and shade, place two coordinating colors of acrylic paints on a disposable plate. Moisten the sponge with water and squeeze out most of the water. Dip the sponge into both paint colors; dab and twist it on the lamp and shade, reapplying paint to the sponge as needed. Let the paint dry.

4 Paint the lamp using the patterns, *right*, for inspiration. The lamp and shade shown, *opposite*, were painted freehand using the same two colors as for sponging. To apply dots, dip a paintbrush handle (for small dots) or the eraser of a pencil (for larger dots) into paint; apply the paint to the lamp base or shade. Let dry.

There's something magical about these tiny toys. Mesmerize little ones with spinning tops that are inexpensive and quick to make—plus oodles of fun to paint!

supplies

Pencil; ruler
³⁄₁₆-inch dowel
Small saw
Drill with ³⁄₁₆-inch bit
¼×2½-inch wood disk
10mm wood beads
Pliers; fine sandpaper
All-purpose sealer
Transfer paper; tracing paper
Scissors; masking tape
Permanent black marker
  or black paint and fine
  paintbrush
Paintbrushes
Acrylic paints in desired colors
¾- and 1-inch-diameter
  wood wheel
Wood glue
Drinking glass
Clear spray varnish

what to do

1 Mark and cut dowel into 2½-inch sections. Drill a hole at the center of the disk. While holding a bead with pliers, widen one end of hole using the drill.

2 Sand all wood parts. Apply sealer to all pieces; let the sealer dry.

3 From transfer paper cut a 2½-inch circle. Transfer a design, *right*, to tracing paper and cut out circle. Place transfer paper on a disk. Place the tracing paper with design on the transfer paper; tape in place. Trace all pattern lines; remove papers from disk.

4 For designs with black outlines, draw outlines with a permanent marker or paint and a fine paintbrush.

5 Fill in design areas with the colors shown on the pattern, or choose different color combinations. Paint the beads, wheels, and two-thirds of the dowel.

6 To assemble the top, insert the dowel through the center of the disk. Apply glue around the dowel on the underside of the disk. Slip on the 1-inch wheel, flat side facing the disk. Apply glue around the dowel that protrudes from the wheel. Place the flat side of the ¾-inch wheel to face the 1-inch wheel. Place a small amount of glue in the hole of the bead; position on the tip of the dowel. To check whether the top spins and the stem is straight, turn it right side up and rotate it slowly.

7 Place top upside down in a drinking glass to let the glue dry. If desired, coat the top with clear spray varnish. Let the varnish dry.

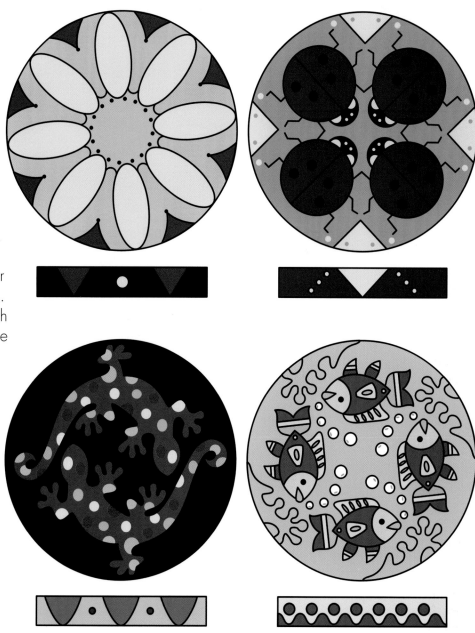

WHIRLING, TWIRLING TOPS PATTERNS

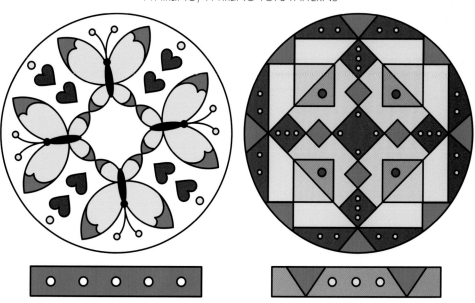

269

Serve a helping of pure fun! These colorful wood bowls hold everything from wrapped treats to office supplies.

FLOWER PATTERN

supplies

Newspapers
Wood salad bowls
White spray primer
Small cans or disposable cups
Acrylic paints in aqua,
  dark red, grass green,
  lavender, lime green, pink,
  pumpkin, purple, royal blue,
  and yellow
Paintbrushes: medium flat,
  small round, and fine liner
Pencil with round eraser
Tracing or white paper
Scissors
Spray acrylic gloss varnish

EMBELLISHED BOWLS
PATTERNS

what to do

1 In a well-ventilated work area, cover a work surface with newspapers. Place bowls right side up on newspapers. Lightly spray on two coats of primer, allowing ample drying time for each coat. Invert the bowls on small cans or disposable cups. Lightly spray two coats of primer on the undersides of the bowls, allowing ample drying time for each coat.

2 Apply two coats of paint to the insides of the bowls; let each coat dry. Apply two coats of paint to the outside and underside of each bowl; let dry.

3 Refer to the patterns and colors used in the photos, *opposite* and *above,* or use designs and colors that you choose. Draw shapes on bowls with a pencil. For the large flower design, trace and cut out the pattern, *opposite;* trace the pattern to the center of a bowl. Paint the designs; let the paint dry. Outline shapes with a fine liner brush. Paint swirly, wavy, and straight lines with a fine liner brush. Apply dots by dipping a paintbrush handle or pencil eraser in paint and dotting the surface. Let dry.

4 Spray acrylic gloss varnish on the bowls. Note: Use only wrapped foods in the bowls; line the bowls with plastic or glass for unwrapped foods.

*Use heavenly papers to make these
quick-cut dimensional stars. Choose from
the patterns, pages 273–275, for a host
of star combinations.*

supplies

*Tracing paper; pencil
Crafts knife
Assorted one- or two-sided
  decorative papers
Ruler; glue stick
Needle and thread
Gem
Paper punch
Ribbon*

what to do

1 Trace and cut out
patterns, *opposite* and
pages *274–275*, from
tracing paper. Trace patterns
to decorative papers (either
two-sided or two coordinating
sheets adhered together).
Cut out the shapes with a
crafts knife and ruler.

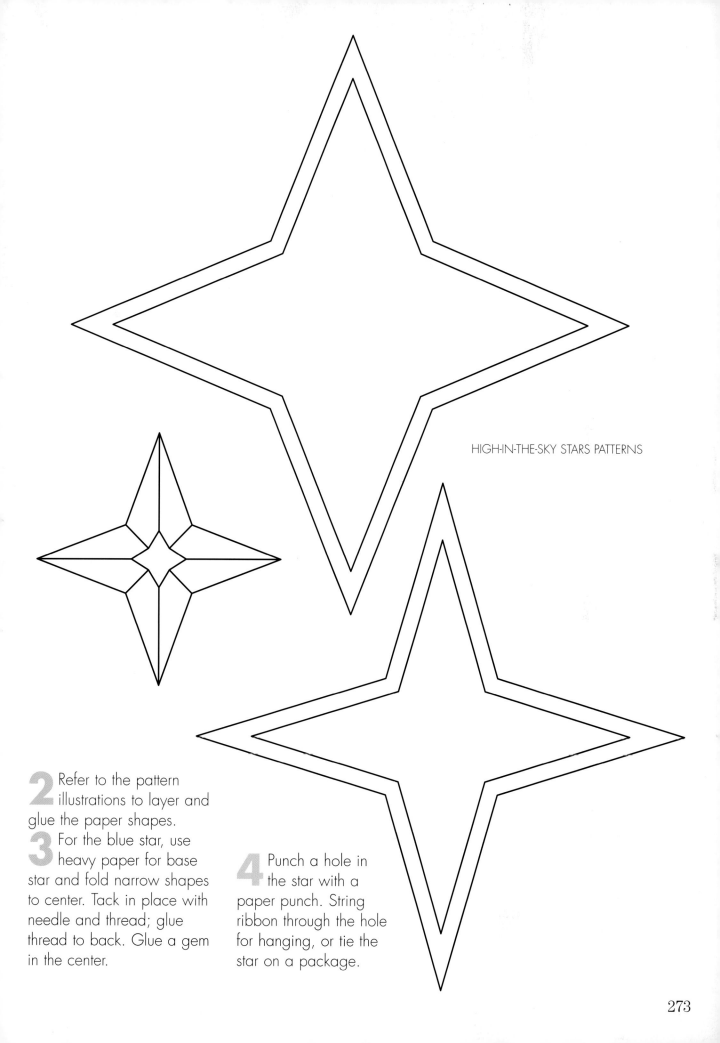

HIGH-IN-THE-SKY STARS PATTERNS

HIGH-IN-THE-SKY STARS PATTERNS

2 Refer to the pattern illustrations to layer and glue the paper shapes.

3 For the blue star, use heavy paper for base star and fold narrow shapes to center. Tack in place with needle and thread; glue thread to back. Glue a gem in the center.

4 Punch a hole in the star with a paper punch. String ribbon through the hole for hanging, or tie the star on a package.

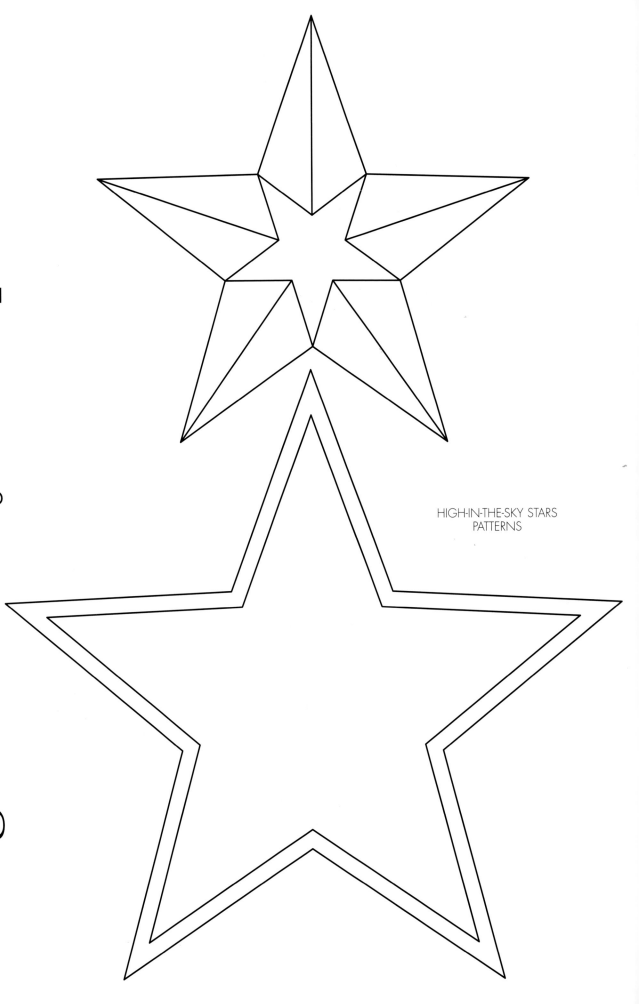

HIGH-IN-THE-SKY STARS
PATTERNS

HIGH-IN-THE-SKY STARS
PATTERNS

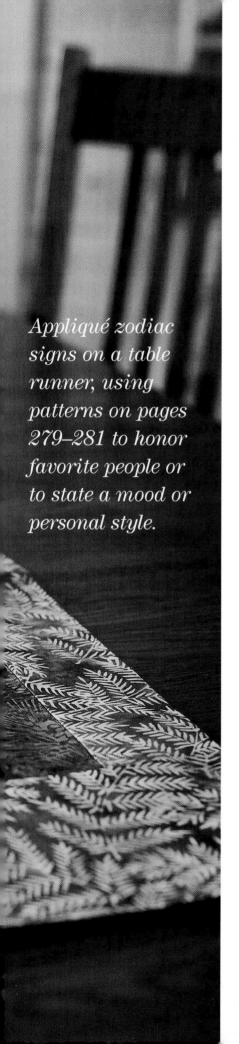

Appliqué zodiac signs on a table runner, using patterns on pages 279–281 to honor favorite people or to state a mood or personal style.

supplies

1½ yards fabric for center and backing; scissors
Measuring tape
6 zodiac blocks
½ yard fabric for borders

Finished size 15½x54½ inches

what to do

1 From fabric cut a 10½x44-inch rectangle for the table runner center. Cut out and layer six zodiac blocks using the photos, *right* and *page 278,* for inspiration and the patterns, *pages 279–281.* Fuse or baste the blocks on the center. Hand- or machine-appliqué in place.

2 Cut two borders 3¼x44 inches; sew to the long sides of the center. Cut two borders 5½x16 inches; sew to each end.

3 Cut a backing 16x55 inches. Right sides facing, sew the backing to the front, leaving an opening for turning. Turn to right side; hand-stitch the opening closed. Press.

VIRGO

CAPRICORN

PISCES

LEO

LIBRA

AQUARIUS

SCORPIO

ARIES

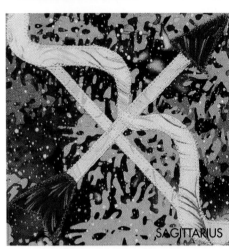

SAGITTARIUS

CANCER

GEMINI

TAURUS

signs

try these ideas

4 more ways to use the signs patterns:

- *Transfer the patterns to the center of a 12-inch square, color with fabric paints, and make into a pillow.*
- *Transfer the appropriate design onto scrapbook papers and cut out. Put on the front of a birthday card.*
- *Transfer the 12 patterns onto a wall in a circle. Paint with wall paints.*
- *Transfer the patterns onto a square of wood. Using a band saw, cut the shapes into puzzle pieces.*

CAPRICORN   PISCES

SCORPIO   LEO

SIGNS OF THE TIMES PATTERNS

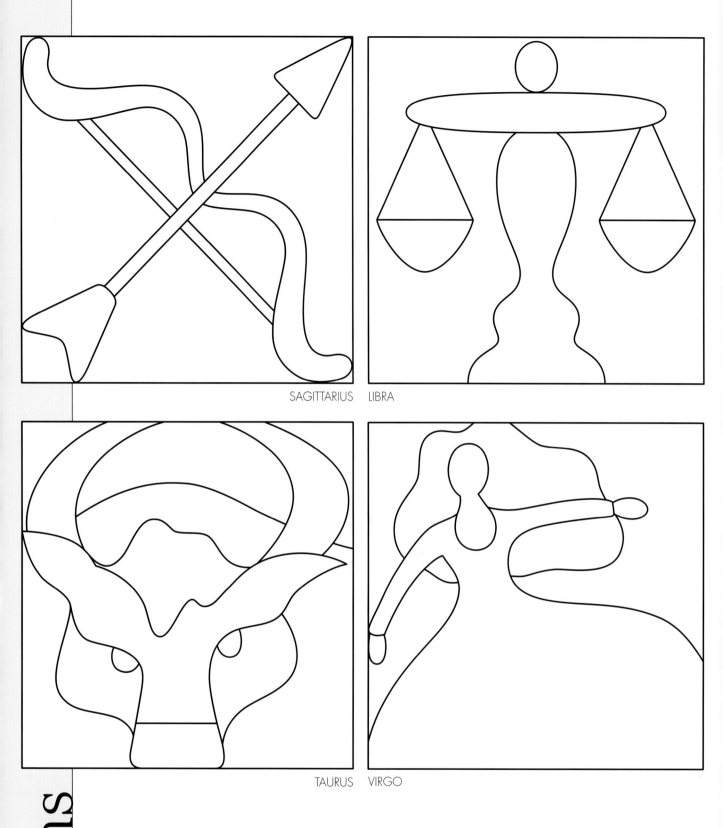

SAGITTARIUS   LIBRA

TAURUS   VIRGO

SIGNS OF THE TIMES PATTERNS

signs

AQUARIUS   ARIES

GEMINI   CANCER

281

how to use the patterns

TRANSFERRING PATTERNS

There are many methods of transferring patterns to create your projects. Here are some methods you'll find easy to master. Whether you're transferring the main outline of a design or adding intricate details, the patterns will guide you to picture-perfect results.

Before You Transfer

Trace the outlines of the design using a pencil and tracing paper. If you wish to change the pattern a bit, move the tracing paper around the pattern to rearrange, add, or subtract elements as desired. If you wish to use the pattern exactly as it is, you may photocopy it for personal use.

Transfer Paper Method

Apply the pattern with commercial transfer paper. Check at local crafts stores or art-supply stores for special artist's transfer paper—several brands are available. Slide the sheet of transfer paper, treated side down, between the pattern and the desired surface, and trace over the lines. Although it might be tempting to substitute carbon paper for the transfer paper, don't. Over time it will bleed through paint or other substances.

Pencil Method

Rub the back of the pattern with a No. 2 pencil. With the traced pattern facedown, hold the pencil horizontally on the paper while applying the graphite. Lightly wipe off the excess graphite dust. Then place the pattern, treated side down, on the surface and retrace the lines with a stylus or pencil.

Chalk Method

Turn the traced pattern facedown, and retrace the lines with a chalk pencil or rub the back with chalk. Then position the pattern, chalk side down, on the surface. Using a stylus or pencil, retrace the lines. Apply very little pressure, or you'll make grooves on the surface.

Make-It-Yourself Transfer Paper

To make your own transfer paper, you'll need tracing paper and several pieces of chalk, both white and colored. To make light sheets of transfer paper (to use on medium- and dark-colored surfaces), rub one side of each piece of tracing paper completely with a piece of inexpensive white chalk, not artist's pastel chalk. Rub the chalk into the paper with your fingers. Then shake off any excess chalk. For dark sheets of transfer paper, use colored chalk or a pencil. Shake off any excess chalk or graphite. Store the sheets by folding the treated sides together.

TRANSFERRING TIPS

- When transferring a pattern, place a sheet of waxed paper on top of it to help you keep track of lines already traced. The stylus will etch the wax paper as you work, showing clearly where you've traced.
- To remove chalk or transfer-paper pattern lines after painting, rub off marks with a soft cloth dampened with clean water. Graphite or other commercial transfer papers may require mineral spirits.
- When tracing a design, a light box makes the process extremely simple. The light makes the design easy to see, and the flat,

horizontal surface is comfortable to draw on. A sunlit window can also be used, but is not as comfortable.

ENLARGING OR REDUCING PATTERNS

As stated on *page 2*, you have permission to photocopy any of the designs in this book for personal use. If you want a copy of a design the same size as printed in this book, photocopy it at 100 percent. Note that some photocopiers will not match the size perfectly.

A photocopy half of the original size would be copied at 50 percent, twice as big would be 200 percent and so on. If you want a particular size and are not sure what percentage to enlarge or reduce the pattern, ask for help at the photocopy center. They should have a proportion wheel on hand to help you calculate the percentage.

USING THE PATTERNS

While we have given you specific crafts project ideas using many of the full-size patterns, keep in mind that the patterns can be combined, altered, enlarged, reduced, and used for a variety of projects and crafting techniques. Use your imagination to adapt the vast selection of patterns to fit your purpose. Because there are hundreds of patterns in the book, the handy index on *pages 284–287* will help you find the perfect pattern.

ALTERNATE PATTERNS

Each project in the book includes the patterns to re-create the craft just as it appears in the photograph. As a bonus, we've added hundreds of alternate interchangeable patterns so you can pick your favorites. And remember, you can reduce or enlarge a pattern from another project to suit a particular project—the sky's the limit!

CHOOSING YOUR PALETTE

Sometimes the patterns are provided in color to give you ideas for coloring in your projects. Sometimes the patterns are in black and white so you can choose your own colors. And sometimes we've given you the black and white patterns reduced in color to give you creative ideas on how the pattern would look using different color variations. You'll soon find that your color choices affect the outcome of a craft and make it personally yours.

STORING THE PATTERNS

Once you've made a pattern, whether a photocopy or a tracing, you may want to keep it for later use. Place the piece or pieces in an envelope and label it with the subject as well as the page number of the book where the design appeared. Keep the envelopes in an alphabetical file for easy reference.

IDEAS, IDEAS, IDEAS

Maybe you've found a pattern that grabs your attention and gets your creative juices flowing, but the project isn't quite what you had in mind. Be sure to read the listings throughout the book describing other ways to use the patterns. You may just find the inspiration you need!

index

continued on page 286

sources and credits

ADHESIVES
Aleene's
www.duncancrafts.com

Centis
Centis Consumer Products
Division
888/236-8476

Elmer's Glue Stick
800/848-9400
www.elmers.com
E-mail:
comments@elmers.com

BUTTONS
Le Bouton Buttons
Blumenthal Lansing Co.
563/538-4211
563/538-4243 (fax)
E-mail:
sales@buttonsplus.com

FABRICS
Bali, Inc.—Princess Mirah
Design
800/783-4612
www.balifab.com
E-mail: batik@balifab.com

Clothworks—A Division of
Fabric Sales Co.
www.clothworks-fabric.com

Moda/United Notions
13795 Hutton
Dallas, TX 75234
www.modafabrics.com

P & B Textiles
1580 Gilbreth Rd.
Burlingame, CA 94010
800/852-2327
www.pbtex.com

R.J.R Fabrics
www.rjrfabrics.com

FELT
National Nonwovens
P.O. Box 150
Easthampton, MA 01027

NOTIONS
Collins & Omnigrid, Inc.
Prym-Dritz Corporation
P.O. Box 5028
Spartanburg, SC 29304
www.dritz.com

OPAQUE WRITERS/
WATERPROOF MARKERS
EK Success Ltd.
www.eksuccess.com

PAPERS
Paper Adventures
P.O. Box 04393
Milwaukee, WI 53204
www.paperadventures.com

SCISSORS & PUNCHES
EK Success Ltd.
www.eksuccess.com

Fiskars Scissors
608/259-1649
www.fiskars.com

DESIGNERS
Susan Banker
Heidi Boyd
Carol Field Dahlstrom
Phyllis Dunstan
Donna Chesnut
Alexa Lett
Ginny McKeever
Barbara Sestock
Margaret Sindelar
Jan Temeyer
Alice Wetzel

GRAPHIC ILLUSTRATION
Chris Neubauer Graphics

PHOTOGRAPHY
Peter Krumhardt
Scott Little
Andy Lyons Cameraworks

PHOTOSTYLING
Carol Field Dahlstrom
Donna Chesnut, assistant